A PERFECT 10

Ten Proven, Scrumptious Recipes
for Each Part of Every Meal

TIM MULLIGAN

HIGHPOINT

This edition published by Highpoint Life Books
For information, write to info@highpointpubs.com.

First Edition

ISBN: 978-1-7372886-7-1

Library of Congress Cataloging-in-Publication Data

Mulligan, Tim
A Perfect 10
Ten Proven, Scrumptious Recipes for Each Part of Every Meal

Summary: "Here are 70 tried-and-true recipes, curated over the decades, that could become your new go-to dishes for all meals—breakfast, appetizers and side dishes, salads, entrees, and desserts—and a Thanksgiving menu that could become your staple for years to come!" —Provided by publisher.

ISBN: 978-1-7372886-7-1 (paperback)
1. Cooking

Library of Congress Control Number: 2022904098

Cover and Interior Design by Sarah M. Clarehart
Photo Credits: All food photos taken by Tim Mulligan.
Cover and back jacket photos by Teresa McCann.

Manufactured in the United States of America

Dedication

To my partner Sean, and kids Cadey and Emiel, who have served as my official food tasters decade after decade, as well as my Mother Judy, Aunt Linda, Aunt Pat, Sister Kelli, and all the home cooks in my life who've passed recipes on to me since I was a kid, and also to my foodie posse and partners in kitchen crime Jeff, Tania, Doreen, and Lori.

Table of Contents

INTRODUCTION

I want to be 100 percent honest upfront—I'm not a trained chef or cook. Sure, I've taken numerous cooking classes, and spent many years in the restaurant biz, both as a server and as a manager. I also want to alleviate any expectations you may have that you will learn any new revolutionary culinary techniques from this book.

But...you have my word that what you will get from this book are tried and true recipes, curated over the decades, that should become your new go-to dishes for all meals—breakfast, appetizers/side dishes, salads, entrees, desserts, and a Thanksgiving menu that will become your staple for years to come.

I've been cooking these recipes for years. My partner Sean and I have been together going on two decades, and have raised our two children into their now young adult years. Through it all, I've cooked breakfasts, lunches, snacks, desserts, and dinners for the family pretty much daily—exploring new recipes, perfecting old ones, and carrying on the cooking and culinary traditions I've carried with me since I was a child.

And a unique child I was. I spent my childhood years pretty much cooking for myself and my family. (I can only recall a few recipes

X

from my own mother, which I've updated in this book.) I traded recipes with all of the neighborhood mothers, which continued through my middle school and high school years. And I've kept those recipes, some of which you will find in this book—ones I've borrowed from my best friends' families and my own relatives —mixed in with newer recipes I've either created or tweaked or fine-tuned during my adult years.

My goal with this cookbook is to take the best of the bunch—and present **A Perfect 10** for each meal period—the top-ten recipes in each meal category that I hope will become your own go-tos as well, whether you have friends coming over, you are stumped on what to cook for yourself or your family, or asked to bring a dish to a friend's house. These are recipes I can guarantee will be crowd pleasers—they are easy, tried and true, and ones my own tribe requests over and over again. Feel free to shake the recipes up, substitute plant-based or vegan items where desired. Basically, do what I do: make recipes work for you.

I work full time. I write in my spare time. I've been raising a family—a houseful of kids, pets, and chaos. I'm busy. Yet I've surrounded myself with foodies. We live and breathe cooking, dining out, and traveling with good food as the goal. I hope this collection of recipes makes your life easier and eliminates having to wade through cookbooks and websites when you are a bind. Just grab this one off of the shelf, and let me help you.

BREAKFAST DISHES

What's better than going out for breakfast? I wouldn't know, because my family never eats breakfast. *BOR-ING*. However, I thrive on those times when we have overnight guests and I can pull out the stops and make my favorite meal of the day—breakfast. At least I can get my family to wolf these dishes down when I make them for dinner.

Kick-Ass Chilaquiles

Having lived in San Diego for 17 years, I have had my fair share of chilaquiles. They are definitely my favorite breakfast or brunch dish, and they are so easy to make. The sauce in this dish is a sauce that I've tinkered with for years, and I think it adds just the right amount of spice. You get a double whammy here. I like to top this dish with my favorite way to cook scrambled eggs—low and slow with dollops of cream cheese cooked through. These eggs are super creamy and soft and a perfect topper for these sure-to-please Kick-Ass Chilaquiles.

- ☐ 1 15-oz. can tomato sauce
- ☐ 1 ½ cups beef broth
- ☐ 1 T. chili powder
- ☐ 1 t. cumin
- ☐ ½ t. garlic powder
- ☐ ¼ t. kosher salt
- ☐ 4 T. butter
- ☐ 5 eggs
- ☐ 3 T. cream cheese
- ☐ 1 T. milk
- ☐ ½ bag tortilla chips (about 6 oz.)
- ☐ Cotija cheese, crumbled, for garnish
- ☐ Cilantro, chopped, for garnish

Kick-Ass Chilaquiles *(Continued)*

1. In a large saucepan, combine the tomato sauce, broth, and spices. Heat the sauce to a simmer, and let it cook for 15 minutes. Cut the butter into smaller pieces and stir it into the sauce. Continue stirring until the butter melts and the sauce becomes smooth and unctuous. Turn off the heat and set the sauce aside.

2. Prepare the eggs (you may fry them, but I prefer these perfect scrambled eggs on top): In a small bowl, whisk together the eggs and milk. Melt 1 teaspoon of butter in a saucepan, and then add the egg/milk mixture. Cook over low-medium heat, stirring often. Dot the eggs with the cream cheese and continue to cook, stirring until well cooked, about 6 minutes. Season with salt and pepper.

3. In a mixing bowl, combine the tortilla chips (unbroken) and the sauce, mixing well until the chips are completely covered.

4. Add the chip mix to a serving bowl and top with the scrambled eggs. Scatter the cotija cheese and cilantro over the top, and serve.

Hammed-Up Eggs in Purgatory

What are eggs in purgatory? Eggs in prison? Hell? I read somewhere that the baked eggs in this dish represent "souls" suspended between heaven and the "hell" of a savory tomato sauce. Regardless, this is an awesome dish; it's an Italian version of another favorite breakfast, Shakshuka. The more you amp up the sauce, the more purgatory-like this dish is. Make sure you serve it with some crusty bread for some yummy dipping.

- ☐ 2 T. olive oil
- ☐ 3 cloves garlic, minced
- ☐ 8 oz. diced ham
- ☐ 1 medium onion, diced
- ☐ 1 green bell pepper, very thinly sliced
- ☐ 1 red bell pepper, very thinly sliced
- ☐ ½ t. red pepper flakes
- ☐ 1 c. tomato sauce (or more, your choice!)
- ☐ ¼ c. chopped parsley leaves
- ☐ 5 eggs
- ☐ 2 T. grated Parmesan cheese
- ☐ Some sort of crusty bread for dipping!

Hammed-Up Eggs in Purgatory *(Continued)*

1. Heat the olive oil in a large skillet over medium-high heat. Add the minced garlic and cook until the garlic is toasty and golden, about 4 minutes.

2. Increase the heat to high and add the diced ham, onion, green and red peppers, and red pepper flakes. Cook, stirring, until the ham starts to crisp up and the veggies soften.

3. Add the tomato sauce and ½ cup water, and cook for 6 minutes.

4. Reduce the heat to medium and sprinkle the chopped parsley over the top. Make five little "wells" in the sauce and crack 1 egg into each hole. Sprinkle the entire dish with the cheese.

5. Cover and cook for about 4 minutes, or until the eggs are cooked to your liking.

6. Serve with the crusty bread and dip away!

GOAT Coffee Cake

Everyone needs in their breakfast arsenal at least one great coffee cake recipe, and to me, this coffee cake is possibly the greatest of all time (GOAT)! It's the easiest way to wow any breakfast guests you have in your home, or make an impression if you are asked to bring a dish to a host's house. I've made countless coffee cakes over the years — I was obsessed with making coffee cake as a child (yes, I was odd) — and this is the one I rely on when in a pinch. The cereal topping is so addicting!

Topping

- ☐ ½ c. corn flakes cereal
- ☐ 1 T. melted butter
- ☐ ¾ c. flour
- ☐ ⅔ c. brown sugar
- ☐ 1 t. cinnamon
- ☐ ½ t. kosher salt
- ☐ 5 T. softened butter

Cake

- ☐ 2 c. flour
- ☐ 1 t. baking powder
- ☐ ½ t. baking soda
- ☐ ½ t. kosher salt
- ☐ 8 T. (1 stick) softened butter
- ☐ 1 c. sugar
- ☐ 2 eggs
- ☐ 2 t. vanilla
- ☐ 1 c. sour cream
- ☐ ⅔ c. blueberry jam

GOAT Coffee Cake *(Continued)*

1. Preheat the oven to 350 degrees. Line an 8 x 8-inch baking dish with foil, leaving a slight overhang. Coat the foil with baking spray.

2. Make the topping: Place the cereal in a bag and crush well. Pour the crushed cereal into a small bowl with the 1 tablespoon of melted butter and mix well. Combine the cereal mixture with the remaining ingredients, smushing the mixture with your hands into a clump-like, crumbly topping.

3. Make the cake batter: Whisk the flour, baking powder, baking soda, and salt in a large bowl. In a separate large bowl, beat the softened butter and the sugar with an electric mixer until fluffy, about 3 minutes. Add the eggs, one at a time, beating well after each

addition. Beat in the vanilla. On low speed, beat the dry ingredients into the mixture. Add the sour cream and beat until you have a thick batter.

4. Spread half of the batter into the prepared baking dish, pushing the batter to the edges. Spoon the jam over the batter and spread it evenly. Add the remaining batter and smooth it out evenly.

5. Scatter the topping on top. Bake until the topping is browned and the cake is not jiggly in the middle, about 65 minutes.

6. Let the cake cool for about 30 minutes, then lift it out of the pan by the foil overhang and let it cool completely on a wire rack.

Bomb Diggity Breakfast Strata

4

SERVES
6-8

If you have a houseful of guests and need to have breakfast on the table in the morning, then a strata is the way to go. Prepare it the night before, cover with plastic wrap, and let the bread soak into the egg mixture all night in the refrigerator. In the morning, bake it in the oven. It's always a crowd pleaser. As for ingredients, you can basically throw in anything you have in your deli or veggie drawer—up to you—but this is a standard variation I make all the time.

- [ ] 10 eggs
- [ ] 3 c. half and half
- [ ] 1 ½ t. kosher salt
- [ ] ¼ c. chopped fresh basil
- [ ] ¼ c. chopped fresh oregano
- [ ] 1 T. butter
- [ ] 1 kielbasa (turkey, pork, or vegan), diced
- [ ] Loaf of challah bread, cut into small 1-in. cubes (about 6 c.)
- [ ] 2 c. shredded Monterey Jack cheese
- [ ] 1 c. torn baby spinach leaves
- [ ] Hot sauce, for serving

Bomb Diggity Breakfast Strata *(Continued)*

1. Prepare the custard: Whisk the eggs, half and half, and salt in a large bowl. Stir in the herbs.

2. Melt the butter in a saucepan, and then sauté the kielbasa, browning slightly. Set aside.

3. Scatter half of the bread cubes into a buttered 13 x 9-inch baking dish.

4. Sprinkle 1 ½ cups of the cheese on top, followed by the spinach leaves. Add the kielbasa on top, and then the remaining bread cubes.

5. Pour the custard over the top, ensuring all of the bread cubes are soaked.

6. Cover the dish with plastic wrap, and let it sit overnight in the fridge.

7. In the morning, preheat the oven to 325 degrees.

8. Uncover the strata and sprinkle the remaining cheese on top.

9. Bake until puffed and set, about 50 minutes. Let the strata rest for 10 minutes before serving. Serve with a bottle of hot sauce on the side.

Bangin' Breakfast Pizzettas

A must-have ingredient everyone should have in their freezers, and learn to love, is frozen puff pastry. You can literally cut it into squares, make a tart shell, and put anything on it. It looks so fancy, and it tastes great! Breakfast is the obvious use of these shells, and this ingredient is a simple variation of a breakfast pizza. Feel free to change up the cheeses and add other items—no matter how you prepare it, it will be a showstopper.

- ☐ 1 sheet of frozen puff pastry, thawed
- ☐ 2 slices Havarti cheese
- ☐ ½ c. grated Parmesan cheese
- ☐ 4 eggs
- ☐ Kosher salt
- ☐ Ground black pepper
- ☐ 4 strips of bacon, cooked and crumbled into pieces
- ☐ Chopped chives, for garnish

Bangin' Breakfast Pizzettas *(Continued)*

1. Preheat the oven to 425 degrees.

2. Line a baking sheet with parchment paper.

3. Unroll the puff pastry sheet and cut it into four even squares. Crimp the squares around the edges, making a kind of tart shell.

4. Transfer the shells to the baking sheet, and pierce them all over with a fork. Bake the shells until golden brown, about 10 minutes.

5. Remove the shells from the oven and let them cool slightly. If they are all puffed up, press down in the middle, gently, with a spoon. In the middle of each shell, place one half of a Havarti slice and sprinkle Parmesan cheese on top of each.

6. Carefully crack 1 egg into the center of each shell. Season the eggs with salt and pepper.

7. Sprinkle the bacon pieces over the top of each shell.

8. Bake for about 12 minutes, or until the egg whites are well set.

9. Sprinkle with the chopped chives and serve!

Ahoy Cap'n Crunch® Pancakes!

When our kids were little and I had a little bit of time in the morning (i.e., weekends!), I would often make standard pancakes from a mix and add some fun surprises. Chocolate chips were, of course, a hit, as were various types of cereal, bananas, blueberries…you name it. This recipe takes it to another level, adding a whole cereal flavor and crunch to the mix, as well as a milky syrup topped with more cereal. It's so fun, and good, and easy to make.

Milk Syrup

- ☐ ½ c. heavy cream
- ☐ 1 c. sweetened condensed milk
- ☐ Pinch of kosher salt

Pancakes

- ☐ 1 c. Cap'n Crunch® cereal
- ☐ 1 c. flour
- ☐ 1 ½ t. sugar
- ☐ 1 t. kosher salt
- ☐ 1 T. baking powder
- ☐ 1 ¼ c. milk
- ☐ 2 eggs
- ☐ 6 T. melted butter
- ☐ Powdered sugar, for garnish

Ahoy Cap'n Crunch® Pancakes! *(Continued)*

1. Make the milk syrup: Combine all of the ingredients and mix well. Set aside.

2. Make the pancakes: Pulse the cereal in a mini-food processor until well crumbled. In a medium bowl, add the ground cereal, flour, sugar, salt, and baking powder and mix well.

3. In a separate mixing bowl, stir together the milk, eggs, and melted butter.

4. Add the wet mixture to the dry mixture, and mix until it is just combined. (Don't go crazy mixing it.)

5. On a griddle set at medium heat, drop the batter by large, consistent spoonfuls, and cook for a few minutes on each side until lightly browned.

6. Serve with soft butter, the milk syrup, a handful of cereal pieces, and a dusting of powdered sugar on top.

Good Ol' Eggs in da Hole

Egg in a Hole is so easy and basic, I almost didn't include it. But how could I not when it's the breakfast dish I make the most, and it's so good and simple? There are many variations of this recipe—use a donut, a tortilla, you name it—but this is my tried-and-true happy place breakfast. Any bread will work; however, thick-cut brioche is the way to go. The brown sugar baked onto the brioche is awesome. If you want, you can substitute the sugar with any seasoned salt for a more savory dish.

- ☐ 2 thick slices of brioche bread
- ☐ 1 T. butter
- ☐ 2 eggs
- ☐ 2 t. brown sugar
- ☐ Kosher salt

Good Ol' Eggs in da Hole *(Continued)*

1. Preheat the oven to 450 degrees.

2. Cut a 1-inch hole in the center of both pieces of bread.

3. In a large ovenproof frying pan, melt the butter. Add the bread and cook until browned.

4. Flip the bread and carefully crack 1 egg into the hole in each piece of bread. Quickly sprinkle the bread with the brown sugar.

5. Immediately put the entire frying pan in the oven and bake until the egg whites set, but the yolk is still runny, about 7 minutes.

6. Remove the pan from the oven, sprinkle the eggs with salt, and serve.

Eggcellent Huevos Rancheros

Having lived so many years in San Diego, as with chilaquiles, we've had our fair share of huevos rancheros. I like this recipe because it is super easy—and I love the bacon-forward sauce it produces. You really can't go wrong here, especially with a nice side of homemade refried beans as an accompaniment.

- ☐ ½ white onion, chopped
- ☐ 2 T. minced garlic
- ☐ 1 t. cumin
- ☐ ½ t. coriander
- ☐ 2 15.5-oz. cans pinto beans, drained and rinsed
- ☐ ¼ c. coconut oil
- ☐ 1 c. chicken stock
- ☐ 1 T. fresh lime juice
- ☐ 12 strips of bacon
- ☐ ½ large white onion, diced
- ☐ ½ green bell pepper, diced
- ☐ 1 jalapeno chili, diced
- ☐ 1 8-oz. can tomato sauce
- ☐ 8 eggs
- ☐ Cheddar cheese, grated, for garnish
- ☐ 8-10 warm tortillas for serving

Eggcellent Huevos Rancheros *(Continued)*

Prepare the refried beans:

1. Heat the coconut oil in a cast-iron skillet over medium heat.

2. Add the chopped white onion and cook until softened, about 3 to 4 minutes.

3. Stir in the cumin, coriander, garlic, and a pinch of salt, and cook for 1 minute.

4. Add the beans and chicken stock and bring to a boil.

5. Cook until the stock has reduced by half and the mixture has thickened up, about 6 minutes.

6. Remove from the heat and mash up the beans the best you can with a large spoon or a potato masher. If you need to thin them, add a little stock to get a thick but stirrable consistency.

7. Stir in the lime juice and add a pinch of salt.

Prepare the bacon and eggs:

1. Follow the directions to make refried beans, on previous page.

2. Heat a large frying pan over medium-high heat. Add the bacon and cook until crisp. Remove the bacon from the pan onto a plate lined with a paper towel. Crumble the bacon into small pieces.

3. To the bacon grease still in the pan, add the diced onion, green pepper, and jalapeno, and cook about 4 minutes, stirring often until softened.

4. Stir in the tomato sauce, along with ½ cup water. Bring to a simmer and let the sauce cook for about 10 minutes. Stir in the bacon pieces.

5. While the sauce is cooking, fry up the eggs to your liking.

6. To serve, place a few tortillas on each plate. Top with 2 eggs. Spoon the sauce over the eggs and sprinkle a little cheese on top. Serve with the refried beans on the side.

Pear Walnut Chocolate Breakfast Loaf

Here's my favorite quick-and-easy breakfast loaf. Yes, you read the recipe correctly—you take a grater and grate a pear. The pear adds fantastic flavor and a moist element to the bread. You could literally substitute any fruit, any nuts, any other add-ins…but this is a combo I think works well and wows the crowd. Also, you can skip the glaze and wrap these loaves up as holiday gifts in mini loaf pans.

Bread

☐ 1 ¼ c. flour

☐ ¾ c. sugar

☐ 1 t. baking powder

☐ 1 t. kosher salt

☐ ½ t. baking soda

☐ 1 t. cinnamon

☐ ½ t. nutmeg

☐ ¾ c. chopped walnuts

☐ ¾ c. mini chocolate chips

☐ 2 eggs

☐ ½ c. vegetable oil

☐ ½ c. plain yogurt

☐ 1 t. vanilla extract

☐ 1 pear, grated

Glaze

☐ 3 T. butter

☐ ½ c. powdered sugar

☐ 1 T. milk

Pear Walnut Chocolate Breakfast Loaf *(Continued)*

1. Preheat the oven to 350 degrees. Spray or lightly butter a standard 9-inch loaf pan, or three mini loaf pans.

2. Prepare the bread: In a medium mixing bowl, combine the flour, sugar, baking powder, salt, baking soda, cinnamon, and nutmeg. Stir in the walnuts and chocolate chips.

3. In a large mixing bowl, whisk together the eggs, oil, yogurt, and vanilla. Mix well. Stir in the grated pear.

4. Combine the two mixtures, stirring until just combined.

5. Spread the batter into the loaf pan and bake for about 55 minutes (or 35 minutes for mini loaves). Let it cool completely before removing it from the pan.

6. Prepare the glaze: Melt the butter over low heat until just browned. Let the butter cool slightly. Whisk in the powdered sugar and milk. Once it becomes a smooth glaze consistency, drizzle it over the bread and serve.

Apple Poppy Seed Muffins

When all else fails, make a bunch of muffins on a Sunday and let them do the trick for your family's on-the-go breakfast for the week. Or, make a bunch, freeze them, and pull them out when you know you have overnight guests. This is my go-to muffin recipe—you can swap out the apples with any fruit, really, but I like the apple and poppy seed combo. Soooooo good warm with butter!

- ☐ 1 egg
- ☐ ¼ c. sugar
- ☐ ¼ c. brown sugar
- ☐ 6 T. melted butter
- ☐ ¾ c. sour cream
- ☐ 1 ½ c. flour
- ☐ ¾ t. baking powder
- ☐ ¾ t. baking soda
- ☐ ¼ t. cinnamon
- ☐ ¼ t. nutmeg
- ☐ ¼ t. kosher salt
- ☐ 2 T. poppy seeds
- ☐ 2 c. peeled and diced apples

Apple Poppy Seed Muffins *(Continued)*

1. Preheat the oven to 375 degrees. Butter a standard 12-muffin tin.

2. In a medium mixing bowl, whisk the egg and both sugars together. Whisk in the melted butter and sour cream.

3. In a separate mixing bowl, mix together the flour, baking powder, baking soda, cinnamon, nutmeg, salt, and poppy seeds. Mix well. Add the dry mixture to the egg mixture and stir until well combined. Stir in the diced apple.

4. Divide the batter among the muffin tins. Bake for about 15 minutes or until golden brown.

5. Let the muffins cool for a few minutes and then remove them from the tin and serve!

APPETIZERS/SIDES

What do you bring when someone asks you to contribute a "side dish"? Of the millions of appetizers out there, which ones stand out? My goal in these situations is to bring a small but mighty starter that is capable of stealing the entire show — giving everyone something to talk about — not just your average veggies and dips, or hummus and chips, or chips and salsa. These recipes will put you on the map.

Tracy's Killer Diller Hot Artichoke Dip

Everybody needs some version of a hot artichoke dip recipe. I was at a work party a few years back when I came upon this version made by my good friend Tracy. I couldn't stop eating it. I tweaked the recipe slightly...I spiced it up a bit...and I am confident this will be the one to keep. Throw the others out!

- ☐ 1 c. mayonnaise
- ☐ 1 c. sour cream
- ☐ 2 c. grated Parmesan cheese
- ☐ 1 14-oz. can chopped artichoke hearts
- ☐ 8 cloves crushed garlic
- ☐ ½ c. sliced black olives
- ☐ ½ t. crushed red pepper flakes
- ☐ ½ t. black pepper
- ☐ Smoked paprika

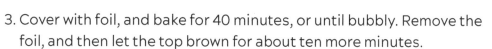

1. Preheat oven to 350 degrees.

2. Mix all ingredients together completely, and then transfer to a lightly greased baking dish. Gingerly sprinkle the top with smoked paprika.

3. Cover with foil, and bake for 40 minutes, or until bubbly. Remove the foil, and then let the top brown for about ten more minutes.

4. Serve warm with crostini, crackers, or veggies...or all of the above. Enjoy!

Quintessential Slow Cooker Buffalo Chicken Dip

Who doesn't love anything with buffalo sauce? I constantly crave the spicy red sauce with some invasion of blue cheese. Really, anything tastes better with buffalo sauce. There are a million versions of buffalo chicken dip out there, but this is my go-to. It's one I've perfected over the years as I tinker with it, and I love that I can literally just dump a simple list of ingredients into my best friend, the slow cooker, and let it do the hard work. Just stir a few times, especially at the end, and you have the yummiest dip out there, perfect for Oscar parties, sporting events, and, yes, binge eating. Dip away!

☐ 2 8-oz. packages cream cheese
☐ 2 c. chopped cooked chicken
☐ 2 c. mild cheddar cheese
☐ 1 c. buttermilk
☐ ⅓ c. hot sauce
☐ 1 T. flour
☐ 1 t. Worcestershire sauce
☐ 1 t. cayenne pepper

☐ 1 t. onion powder
☐ 1 t. garlic powder
☐ 1 leek, thinly sliced
☐ Handful of chopped parsley
☐ ¼ c. blue cheese crumbles
☐ Crackers, celery, and carrot sticks for dipping

1. Place all ingredients, except the parsley and blue cheese into a slow cooker. Mix well.

2. Cook, covered, on a high setting for 2 hours. The dip will be bubbly and well melted. Stir until the dip is very smooth and combined well.

3. Sprinkle with the parsley and blue cheese, reduce to a warm setting, and serve with crackers, celery, and carrot sticks.

Hypercharged Grilled Halloumi Cheese and Watermelon Stacks

Grilled halloumi cheese makes a perfect vessel for any sort of dip, salad, or topping — it's really the perfect appetizer ingredient. Besides being sturdy and able to withstand a reception/cocktail party without making a mess, it tastes great — salty and slightly tangy. It also makes a great substitute for meat in most recipes. But marinated and topped with watermelon…heaven!

- ☐ 1 t. dried minced onion
- ☐ 1 t. minced garlic
- ☐ Pinch of kosher salt
- ☐ ¼ c. red wine vinegar
- ☐ 1 T. honey
- ☐ ½ c. olive oil
- ☐ 3 T. chopped pistachios
- ☐ 2 T. chopped fresh mint
- ☐ 12 small wedges watermelon, rind and seeds removed (you can substitute cantaloupe slices also)
- ☐ 12 oz. halloumi cheese, cut into 12 slices

1. Place the onion and garlic into a medium mixing bowl and throw in a pinch of kosher salt. Add the vinegar and honey, whisking as you go.

2. Slowly whisk in the olive oil, and then stir in the pistachios and mint.

3. Place the watermelon slices in a shallow dish. Pour the dressing over the top, and let it marinate in the refrigerator, covered, for at least 1 hour.

4. Heat a large skillet over medium heat and coat with cooking spray or about 1 tablespoon of olive oil. Add the halloumi slices and cook for about 1 minute on each side, or until each side is lightly browned. Remove the cheese from the pan.

5. Top each halloumi slice with a piece of the marinated watermelon and serve.

Da Bomb Hot Peanut Sesame Dip

My Aunt Linda loves to say she's not the best in the kitchen, which may or may not be true. But two of my favorite recipes in this book came from her, recipes she doesn't even recall giving to me years and years ago. (See the Wyoming Whopper Cookies recipe on p. 151) This dip ... I swear once you start eating it, you will be hooked and not be able to contain yourself. So easy to make, and soooooo good. I've been putting it out at cocktail parties for over 30 years now. Thanks, Linda!

- ☐ ²/₃ c. chunky peanut butter
- ☐ 6 cloves garlic, minced
- ☐ 2 T. soy sauce
- ☐ 3 T. chili oil
- ☐ 1 T. sesame oil
- ☐ 2 T. lemon juice
- ☐ 3 T. sugar
- ☐ Veggies or crackers for dipping

1. In a small mixing bowl, mix all ingredients together and let the mixture sit out for at least 2 hours.

2. Serve with veggies or crackers. It's amazing!

Pineapple Fried Rice for the Ages

Fried rice is so easy. You can really throw any proteins, veggies, and spice into this basic recipe and have an awesome result every time. I made this dish all through college, since it's something one can really make last a long time on a budget. I like this version with pineapple, ham, and a spicy Asian sauce (I'm a bit obsessed with gochujang sauce). It is so easy and so delicious!

- ☐ 2 T. vegetable oil
- ☐ 3 eggs, slightly beaten
- ☐ 1 c. diced ham (you can also use linguica, pancetta, Canadian bacon...)
- ☐ Kosher salt
- ☐ 3 c. cooked rice (I use brown, but this is your choice)

- ☐ 1 c. pineapple tidbits
- ☐ 3 scallions, diced
- ☐ 1 T. Korean gochujang sauce (or regular Asian chili sauce)
- ☐ 1 t. diced ginger
- ☐ Toasted sesame oil

1. Heat 1 tablespoon of the oil in a large wok or skillet over high heat. Add the eggs and swirl around the pan to spread out and coat the pan. Cook for about 15 seconds and then remove the eggs and set aside.

2. Add the ham, season with salt, and stir fry until the ham is slightly crisped and browned, only a few minutes. Remove the ham to a bowl and set aside.

3. Add 1 tablespoon of the oil to the skillet. Add the rice, pineapple, and scallions. Season with a pinch of salt, and then add the gochujang sauce and ginger. Stir fry until the pineapple softens up, about 4 minutes. Return the eggs and ham to the skillet and stir well, incorporating and breaking up the eggs throughout the dish.

4. Serve in a bowl topped with the remaining scallions and a few dashes of toasted sesame oil.

Crispy Brussels Sprouts... with Cooked Grapes!

Oh, how I hated Brussels sprouts as a kid when we were forced to eat them steamed, whole. So gross. I never would have guessed as a kid that not only would they one day take the food world by storm, but also they'd become my favorite food, as well as my kids' favorite food. We must eat them at least three nights a week. And now, of course, every restaurant has some unique Brussels sprouts recipe on their menus—roasted, fried, sautéed...you name it. I think this recipe is the best of the bunch!

- ☐ 2 lbs. Brussels sprouts, halved
- ☐ 3 T. olive oil
- ☐ ½ t. kosher salt
- ☐ Freshly ground black pepper
- ☐ 3 T. unsalted butter
- ☐ 2 c. red seedless grapes, halved
- ☐ 2 t. chopped fresh thyme
- ☐ 3 scallions, chopped
- ☐ 2 T. hot honey
- ☐ ¼ c. chopped nuts (almonds, walnuts, or hazelnuts)

1. Preheat the oven to 450 degrees.

2. In a large bowl, toss the Brussels sprouts with the olive oil, salt, and a few pinches of pepper.

3. Spread the sprouts on a baking sheet and cook 25 to 30 minutes, tossing halfway through. They should be tender and blackened in spots.

Crispy Brussels Sprouts... with Cooked Grapes! *(Continued)*

4. Melt the butter in a large skillet over medium heat. Add the grapes and thyme to the butter and cook, stirring frequently, until the grapes start bursting, about 4 minutes.

5. Add the scallions and hot honey, turn up the heat, and bring the sauce to a boil.

6. Reduce the heat to medium-low and simmer, letting the sauce thicken and grapes caramelize, about 2 minutes. Stir in the chopped nuts and season with salt and pepper.

7. Place the sprouts in a serving dish, then pour the sauce directly on top.

Note: I also love to pick a bunch of leaves off of the sprouts while uncooked, flash fry them, toss them with a little salt, and put them on top for garnish. Yum!

Rockin' Caramelized Onion Dip

This is my go-to party dip that I bring to others' houses—and now people are specifically requesting it. Yes, there are countless numbers of dips that contain a mixture of sour cream, cream cheese, and mayonnaise, but in my opinion, this is one of the best. It's so easy to make caramelized onions, and mixed with these spices, it's simply amazing!

- ☐ 2 T. unsalted butter
- ☐ 2 T. olive oil
- ☐ 2 medium white onions, thinly sliced
- ☐ ½ t. kosher salt
- ☐ 1 t. smoked paprika
- ☐ 1 c. sour cream
- ☐ 4 oz. cream cheese
- ☐ ¼ c. mayonnaise
- ☐ 1 T. red wine vinegar
- ☐ 2 green onions, thinly sliced
- ☐ ¼ t. cayenne pepper
- ☐ Grilled bread (crostini) or crackers for serving

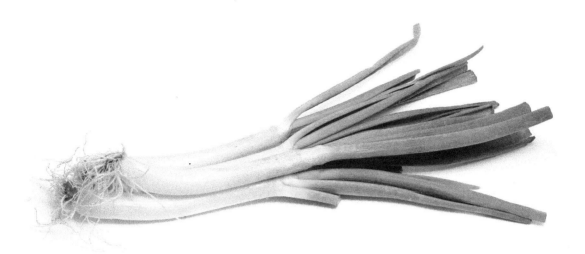

Rockin' Caramelized Onion Dip *(Continued)*

1. In a large skillet over medium heat, heat the butter and olive oil until the butter is melted.

2. Add the sliced onions and season with the salt and smoked paprika. Cook until the onions turn brown and caramelize, stirring often, about 20 minutes. Remove the onions from the heat and transfer them onto a paper towel–lined plate to cool.

3. With an electric mixer, combine the sour cream, cream cheese, mayonnaise, and vinegar until smooth.

4. By hand, stir in about ¾ of the caramelized onions and ¾ of the chopped green onions, along with the cayenne pepper. Season with kosher salt if desired.

5. Transfer to a serving bowl, and top with the remaining caramelized onions and green onions. Serve with grilled bread or crackers.

Party Stoppin' Greek Layered Dip with Pita Chips

I'm a geek when it comes to servingware—and any chance I get to use my favorite glass trifle dish, I go for it. Obviously, trifle dishes are perfect for pretty layered dips, like this crowd-pleasing recipe. Of course, you can also be more ambitious here—hummus is super easy to make from scratch, as are tzatziki and pita chips—or say "screw it" and use store-bought. Just dip away with whatever works!

- ☐ 1 lb. ground beef (or substitute with turkey or plant-based meat)
- ☐ 1 t. garlic salt
- ☐ 2 t. Greek seasoning
- ☐ 1 16-oz. container store-bought hummus
- ☐ 1 ½ c. store-bought tzatziki dip
- ☐ 1 c. shredded iceberg lettuce
- ☐ 2 medium Roma tomatoes, finely chopped
- ☐ ½ red onion, diced
- ☐ ½ c. chopped Kalamata olives
- ☐ 4 oz. crumbled feta cheese
- ☐ Toasted pita bread cut in wedges, or store-bought pita chips, for dipping

1. In a large skillet, brown the beef with the garlic salt and Greek seasoning. Drain and set aside.

2. In a shallow serving dish or trifle dish, spread the hummus on the bottom. Top with a layer of the meat, followed by the tzatziki. Layer on top of that the lettuce, tomatoes, onions, olives, and feta.

3. Serve at room temperature with pita chips.

Super-Easy Cheesy Olive Bread

I love baking, but admittedly, I am not a great bread maker. (I'm a bit afraid of yeast-based baking!) This bread is so good…and so easy. It is perfect on an appetizer buffet, goes awesome with tapenade or any dip, really, and is super-fun to make over the holidays. Just bake it in holiday tins and give it out as gifts. (I delivered a loaf last year to every member of my team.) If you are using mini loaf tins, this recipe will fill three of them. Enjoy!

- ☐ 2 ½ c. flour
- ☐ 1 t. kosher salt
- ☐ 1 ½ t. baking powder
- ☐ ½ t. baking soda
- ☐ ¼ c. olive oil
- ☐ 1 c. plain yogurt
- ☐ 2 eggs
- ☐ 1 c. sliced Kalamata or green olives
- ☐ 2 c. grated cheddar cheese
- ☐ 1 T. chopped fresh oregano
- ☐ ½ t. ground black pepper

Super-Easy Cheesy Olive Bread *(Continued)*

1. Preheat the oven to 350 degrees. Spray or lightly butter a standard 9-inch loaf pan, or three mini loaf pans.

2. In a large mixing bowl, whisk together the flour, salt, baking powder, and baking soda.

3. In a small mixing bowl, whisk together the olive oil and plain yogurt. Once mixed well, whisk in the eggs.

4. Combine the wet mixture to the dry mixture. It will be very thick, gummy, and messy—do your best.

5. Fold in the olives, 1¾ cups of the cheese, oregano, and pepper. (To be honest, I use my greased hands for this step.)

6. Spread the batter into the loaf pan(s), and sprinkle the remaining cheese over the top.

7. Bake the bread until the cheese browns and the top springs back when lightly pressed, about 50 minutes. Serve warm if desired (it's great warm), or let cool and slice and eat throughout the day! If you're going to gift them, they are good for a few days.

Funeral Potatoes

10
SERVES
8-10
(though
you might
eat it all
yourself)

Ahh...funeral potatoes! These have become a mainstay at parties at my place. I whip up a batch early in the day, cover them with foil and hide them in the fridge, and then late in the night I surprise my guests with a late-night carb attack. My guests devour these with hot sauce, usually with a fork right out of the serving dish. This recipe has been floating around for decades—I've slightly tweaked it here. And yes, I prefer the corn flake topping to the also-popular potato chip topping. Debate away!

- [ ] 2 c. sour cream
- [ ] 1 10.5-oz. can cream of chicken soup
- [ ] 10 T. butter
- [ ] 1 t. kosher salt
- [ ] ¼ t. ground black pepper
- [ ] ½ t. mustard powder
- [ ] 2 t. dried minced onion
- [ ] 30 oz. frozen hash brown potatoes, thawed
- [ ] 2 c. shredded cheddar cheese
- [ ] 2 c. corn flakes, crushed

1. Preheat the oven to 350 degrees.

2. In a large mixing bowl, combine the sour cream, soup, 6 tablespoons of melted butter, salt, pepper, mustard powder, and dried onion. Mix well.

Funeral Potatoes *(Continued)*

3. Add the hash browns and cheese, stirring to combine.

4. Spoon the mixture into a 13 x 9-inch baking dish.

5. In a small mixing bowl, combine the crushed corn flakes with 4 tablespoons of melted butter, mixing well. Sprinkle this mixture over the potatoes.

6. Bake uncovered for 45 minutes. The potatoes should be lightly browned and bubbling around the edges.

7. Serve with hot sauce.

SALADS

Ahh...the salad. So many variations, and so many boring ones at that. I love being assigned a salad for a meal or party, and so should you after taking a look at this collection. The trick is to not fall back on store-bought dressings and uninspiring ingredients. This Perfect 10 list is a great mix of what could be standard-fare salads, but amped-up just enough to turn them into true crowd-pleasers. Here I run the gamut on types — from my own take on a standard green salad, to a chop salad, to a pasta salad, and on to a more fruit-forward option. I hope these help you transform your salad game!

Da Best Cucumber Avocado Sesame Salad

Do you struggle with what to bring to that dinner party or event when you've been assigned the vague "side" dish? This one is awesome. Serve it with a protein entrée of your choice — or let it stand on its own as a great lunch or dinner for one or two when you don't want to go nuts cooking. I love it with salmon or an Asian noodle dish. My entire family devours it, and it is definitely on my most-requested list.

- ☐ 2 T. rice vinegar
- ☐ 1 T. mayonnaise
- ☐ ½ t. soy sauce
- ☐ ½ t. sesame oil
- ☐ 2 Persian cucumbers, thinly sliced
- ☐ 3 green onions (scallions), thinly sliced
- ☐ ¼ t. kosher salt
- ☐ 1 avocado, chopped
- ☐ Sesame seeds, for garnish

1. In a medium mixing bowl, whisk the vinegar, mayonnaise, soy sauce, and sesame oil together.

2. Add the cucumbers, scallions, and salt, and mix well.

3. Gently stir in the avocado pieces. (Don't squish them!)

4. Garnish the top with sesame seeds and serve.

Good Old-Fashioned Green Salad

Let's face it, green salads are usually boring. But how many times are we asked what we can bring to an event or dinner party, and the answer is always…"salad." Cringe. Well, cringe no more, because this salad recipe that I've been making for years. Just ask my work teams, for whom I prepare dinner for every holiday. This salad is always requested, and I don't you think you can really say that about most standard green salads. It's a winner you will use over and over again.

- ☐ 2 T. white wine vinegar
- ☐ 2 T. Dijon mustard
- ☐ ¼ t. kosher salt
- ☐ ¼ t ground black pepper
- ☐ 6 T. olive oil
- ☐ 5 oz. mixed fall greens
- ☐ 6 oz. blue cheese crumbles
- ☐ ½ c. candied walnuts (whatever flavor you want!)
- ☐ ½ c. dried cherries

1. Prepare the vinaigrette: In a small bowl, combine the vinegar, mustard, salt, and pepper, and whisk well. Add the olive oil, whisking constantly until emulsified.

2. In a large salad bowl, toss the fall greens, blue cheese, walnuts, and cherries, with 2/3 of the vinaigrette. Season with salt and pepper and add more vinaigrette as needed.

3. Serve immediately.

Melted Cheese Surprise Salad

Yes, this salad is served warm. Yes, it has melted cheese on it. It's so unique, and so different—and perfect for a nice dinner party. I like to mix kale and red leaf lettuce here. You could also throw in some radicchio if you want a little extra bite. It's really good.

- ☐ 3 T. red wine vinegar
- ☐ ¼ c. olive oil
- ☐ Kosher salt
- ☐ Ground black pepper
- ☐ 1 large head red leaf lettuce
- ☐ 5 oz. chopped kale
- ☐ ¼ lb. Manchego cheese, grated
- ☐ 2/3 c. sliced almonds (or pine nuts or hazelnuts)
- ☐ Balsamic vinegar, for drizzling

1. Prepare the dressing: In a small mixing bowl, whisk together the red wine vinegar and olive oil. Season to taste with salt and pepper.

2. In a large mixing bowl, toss the lettuce and kale with the dressing.

3. Place the salad in an oven-proof serving dish and sprinkle the cheese on top. Broil the salad for about 1 minute, or until the cheese is melted. Remove from the oven.

4. Toast the sliced nuts under a broiler or sauté them in butter.

5. Sprinkle the salad with the toasted nuts.

6. Drizzle balsamic vinegar over the top (not too much!) and serve.

Heart-Stopping Warm Spinach Bacon Salad

Though I don't have many recipes in my collection that come from my parents, there is one dish from my stepmother that I always recall fondly—warm spinach salad. I requested this salad all throughout my high school years, and I have kept this recipe close to the chest since then. There's something very "steakhousey" and old-school about it… and it never fails to dazzle. It's best, obviously, for dinner parties at home, because the dressing is served warm right from the skillet.

- ☐ 6 slices bacon
- ☐ ¼ c. white wine vinegar
- ☐ 1 t. honey
- ☐ 1 t. Dijon mustard
- ☐ 2 T. olive oil
- ☐ ¼ t. kosher salt
- ☐ ¼ t. ground black pepper
- ☐ 1 lb. spinach, stems cut off
- ☐ ¼ c. grated Parmesan cheese
- ☐ 2 c. red grapes, cut in half
- ☐ 5 hard-boiled eggs, sliced

1. In a skillet, cook the bacon until very crisp. Remove the bacon to paper towels, keeping the drippings in the pan. Break the bacon into small pieces and set aside.

2. Into the drippings in the warm skillet whisk together the vinegar, honey, mustard, oil, salt, and pepper until emulsified.

3. Place the spinach in a large bowl and pour the warm dressing over the top.

4. Add the cheese, grapes, eggs, and bacon pieces, and toss well. Serve immediately.

Supertastic Melon Mozzarella Salad

I spend a good deal of time in sunny Palm Springs, which means many lunches al fresco. Poolside. And that can create a challenge in finding the right light, fresh meal to prepare and serve. So, a huge thanks to my awesome neighbors in the desert, who turned me onto this great melon ball salad. And who doesn't love using a good old-fashioned melon baller? And also...these baked prosciutto "croutons" are amazing, and you can throw them on literally anything. Let the pool parties commence!

Salad

- ☐ 3 oz. prosciutto, cut into strips
- ☐ ½ watermelon
- ☐ 1 cantaloupe
- ☐ 1 honeydew melon
- ☐ 2 c. cherry tomatoes, halved
- ☐ 1 c. torn basil leaves
- ☐ 8 oz. fresh mozzarella balls (or 8 oz. burrata cheese)
- ☐ ¼ c. toasted pine nuts
- ☐ 2 T. chopped fresh mint leaves

Fig Balsamic Vinaigrette Dressing

- ☐ ¼ c. olive oil
- ☐ 3 T. zucca balsamic vinegar
- ☐ 2 T. fresh lemon juice
- ☐ 2 T. honey
- ☐ 2 t. fig jam
- ☐ Kosher salt
- ☐ Ground black pepper
- ☐ Ground red pepper flakes

Supertastic Melon Mozzarella Salad *(Continued)*

1. Prepare the prosciutto: Preheat the oven to 400 degrees. Line a baking sheet with aluminum foil and lay the prosciutto evenly on the foil. Cook for about 10 minutes, or until crispy.

2. Prepare the salad: Using a melon-baller, carve out as many balls as possible from the watermelon, honeydew melon, and cantaloupe. In a salad bowl, combine the melon balls, tomatoes, and basil.

3. Prepare the dressing: Add all ingredients in a mason jar and shake well to combine. Season to taste with the salt, black pepper, and red pepper flakes.

4. Put it all together: Drizzle half of the dressing over the salad and toss to coat. Add the cheese, toasted pine nuts, and the rest of the dressing.

5. Top with crispy prosciutto and chopped mint leaves. Enjoy!

Killer Chop Salad

During my college years, I worked for a chain of Italian restaurants at three of their locations, and their chop salad was the top seller. Since that time (decades ago!) chop salads have, of course, become de rigueur. You see them everywhere, with some variations on the recipe (though all seem pretty consistent). Here's my recreation of that classic chop salad. It still kills decades later.

Salad

- ☐ 1 c. garbanzo beans, rinsed and chopped
- ☐ ¼ c. basil, finely chopped
- ☐ 1 head iceberg lettuce, chopped
- ☐ 4 oz. mozzarella cheese, grated
- ☐ 4 oz. white cheddar cheese, grated
- ☐ 12 oz. cooked chicken, chopped
- ☐ 8 oz. salami, chopped (I like to use soppressata)
- ☐ 3 Roma tomatoes, chopped
- ☐ 3 large green onions, chopped
- ☐ 1 c. pitted green olives, chopped

Italian Vinaigrette

- ☐ 1 egg yolk
- ☐ 1 T. Dijon mustard
- ☐ 2 T. minced garlic
- ☐ ½ t. mustard powder
- ☐ ½ t. kosher salt
- ☐ ½ t. ground black pepper
- ☐ 2 t. dried oregano
- ☐ ½ t. sugar
- ☐ 3 oz. red wine vinegar
- ☐ 1 c. olive oil
- ☐ 2 T. lemon juice

Killer Chop Salad *(Continued)*

1. Prepare the salad: Toss all salad ingredients well in a large bowl. Make sure you keep some consistency in the size of chop you are employing.

2. Prepare the dressing: Combine the egg yolk, Dijon mustard, garlic, mustard powder, salt, pepper, oregano, and sugar. Whisk well. Whisk in the vinegar. Then slowly whisk in the olive oil and lemon juice.

3. Dress the salad appropriately based on your preference (you will likely have some dressing left over), and let the salivating commence!

Scrumptious Sesame Pasta Salad

There was a time when I was in high school when everyone was making pasta salad. It was everywhere, and a small group of my friends competed with each other to get the best recipe. I don't actually know where I found this one, but I've been making it for over 35 years. It's held up. Yum.

- ☐ 1 18-oz. bag rotelli or fusilli pasta
- ☐ ½ c. olive oil
- ☐ ⅓ c. soy sauce
- ☐ ¼ c. toasted sesame seeds
- ☐ ⅓ c. white wine vinegar
- ☐ 3 T. sugar
- ☐ ½ t. kosher salt
- ☐ ½ t. ground black pepper
- ☐ 3 c. diced cooked chicken
- ☐ ½ c. chopped parsley
- ☐ ½ c. thinly sliced green onion
- ☐ 1 ½ c. torn baby spinach leaves

1. Cook the pasta in salted boiling water per the package directions. Set aside.

2. In a medium mixing bowl, whisk together the oil, soy sauce, sesame seeds, vinegar, sugar, salt, and pepper.

3. Add the dressing, chicken, parsley, green onions, and spinach leaves to the pasta. Mix well.

4. Refrigerate and enjoy chilled.

Supreme Strawberry Summer Salad

This is *the* salad I've been making for holiday dinners for years. People inhale it. The sesame dressing is a winner — it is such a creative use of store-bought Italian dressing. You can put it on anything, but mixed with strawberries, nuts, and cheese…you will rule the night with this simple salad. I think I'll make it right now, just thinking about it!

Sesame Vinaigrette

- ☐ ¼ c. store-bought Italian dressing
- ☐ 1 T. honey
- ☐ 1 T. soy sauce
- ☐ ½ t. sesame oil

Salad

- ☐ 1 5-oz. bag mixed lettuce
- ☐ 1 ½ c. strawberries, halved
- ☐ ½ c. candied/spiced pecans (or walnuts)
- ☐ ¼ c. crumbled feta cheese

1. Prepare the vinaigrette: Pour the Italian dressing into a small mixing bowl. Whisk in the remaining ingredients. Set aside.

2. In a large bowl, mix the lettuce, strawberries, nuts, and feta.

3. Pour the vinaigrette over the salad, toss well to coat all ingredients, and serve. Easy peasy!

Dazzling Bread Salad

What's a Top Ten list of salads without some form of a panzanella? You can substitute whatever you want here, but this is the combo I have perfected over the years. It's great as a free-standing meal, or alongside any sort of protein entrée.

- ☐ 8 c. ciabatta bread, cut into 1-in. cubes
- ☐ 2 lb. chopped tomatoes
- ☐ ½ c. diced fresh basil
- ☐ ½ c. chopped pitted Kalamata olives
- ☐ ½ c. sliced hearts of palm
- ☐ ½ red onion, thinly sliced
- ☐ ⅔ c. salami, cut into small strips
- ☐ 1 8-oz. container of fresh mozzarella cheese balls, halved
- ☐ ¼ c. red wine vinegar
- ☐ 1 t. Dijon mustard
- ☐ ¾ c. olive oil
- ☐ 1 T. lemon zest

1. Place the cubed bread into a large bowl. Toss with the chopped tomatoes and basil.

2. Stir in the olives, hearts of palm, red onion slices, salami, and cheese.

3. In a small mixing bowl, whisk together the vinegar and mustard. Slowly whisk in the oil and lemon zest.

4. Drizzle the dressing over the salad and toss. If not serving right away, this salad can be chilled for a few hours ahead of time.

Orange You Glad You Made This Orange Olive Salad?

Sometimes you don't need a big fancy and hearty salad and want to dazzle your guests with something a bit more *avant-garde* (and easier to produce)! That's why I love this "salad" — it's really just oranges and olives with a lovely little Spanish vinaigrette. Super simple, elegant, and easy to make!

- ☐ 4 oranges (I like Cara Cara oranges)
- ☐ ¼ c. pitted Kalamata olives, quartered
- ☐ ½ t. paprika
- ☐ 2 T. fresh lemon juice
- ☐ 1 T. olive oil
- ☐ 2 T. chopped fresh parsley

1. Peel the oranges. Remove the outer membrane and slice each one into about six slices.

2. Arrange the oranges decoratively on a serving plate or platter. Scatter the olives over the oranges.

3. Prepare the dressing: Combine the paprika and lemon juice, and then whisk in the oil. Stir in the parsley.

4. Drizzle the dressing over the oranges and serve!

SOUPS

I could live on soup. I know, I sound like I'm 40 years older than I really am. But hey, I'm an old soul who loves a good steaming-hot bowl of the stuff. (Sorry, no cold soups found here.) I love to whip up batches of soup on a Sunday and keep them for the week. And yes, I've been known to host soup parties, supplying ingredients and Tupperware®, and sending folks home with their prized creations. You can always find containers of soup in my freezer ready for thawing and enjoying on busy weeknights. I've tried to include all types here — lights to heavies, brothy to thick as all get-out — along with some of the recipes I've been perfecting and preparing for over 40 years now. These truly are the Perfect 10 soup recipes.

Real-Deal Spicy Sausage and Kale Soup

SERVES
4

My kids and I love this soup — and it's perfect for cold weather. Make it on the weekend, and then dole it out all week long. This particular recipe, with its spicy sausage, garbanzos, and wilted kale, is so delicious — hearty, spicy, and addictive. You can, of course, make it vegetarian with plant-based sausage, which I often do, or even use turkey sausage. It's super easy, and a real crowd-pleaser.

- ☐ 2 T. olive oil
- ☐ 1 lb. hot Italian sausage links (casings removed)
- ☐ 1 lb. baby potatoes, cut into small pieces
- ☐ 2 shallots, sliced
- ☐ 1 fennel bulb, diced
- ☐ 2 stalks celery, finely chopped
- ☐ 1 leek, sliced
- ☐ 4 cloves garlic, crushed
- ☐ 2 T. chopped fresh thyme

- ☐ 1 t. crushed red pepper flakes
- ☐ 1 bay leaf
- ☐ Kosher salt
- ☐ 1 qt. chicken stock
- ☐ 1 15-oz. can garbanzo beans, drained and rinsed
- ☐ 1 14.5-oz. can diced tomatoes
- ☐ 5 oz. chopped kale
- ☐ 2 T. fresh lemon juice
- ☐ Croutons, for garnish

1. In a large soup pot, heat the oil over medium-high heat. Add the sausage and cook, stirring often and breaking up the sausage into smaller chunks, until browned, about 5 minutes. Transfer the sausage to a plate.

Real-Deal Spicy Sausage and Kale Soup
(Continued)

2. Add the potatoes, shallots, fennel, celery, leeks, garlic, thyme, red pepper flakes, and bay leaf to the pot, and season well with salt. Partially cover, and cook until the vegetables soften, about 10 minutes.

3. Add the chicken stock, garbanzo beans, and tomatoes. Bring it to a boil, and then add the browned sausage and the kale. Cook for about 4 minutes, stirring often.

4. Stir in the lemon juice, and serve. (I like it with croutons on top!)

Lux Lentil Sausage Soup

If I had to list my family's #1 soup request, it's this one. This recipe is a version I've been making for decades, inspired by a great Italian restaurant I worked at all through law school. Creamy, decadent, and loaded with lentils and sausage, this soup is so good and makes for a great holiday tradition. I always serve it with a spoonful of marinara on the top, and of course, some good crusty bread for dipping. Make double — it goes fast!

- ☐ 20 oz. cooked spicy sausage
- ☐ 4 T. butter
- ☐ 3 c. diced mirepoix (1 c. each white onions, carrots, celery)
- ☐ 2 leeks, chopped (whites only)
- ☐ 6 c. chicken stock
- ☐ 3 c. softened lentils (soak as directed on package)
- ☐ 3 T. Dijon mustard
- ☐ 2 T. red wine vinegar
- ☐ 1½ c. heavy cream
- ☐ 2 t. Kosher salt
- ☐ ½ t. ground black pepper
- ☐ 3 oz. torn spinach leaves
- ☐ Marinara or pizza sauce, for garnish
- ☐ Parmesan cheese, for garnish

Lux Lentil Sausage Soup *(Continued)*

1. In a large soup pot, sauté the sausage, butter, and vegetables until the veggies are well-softened.

2. Add the stock and lentils, and bring to a boil. Reduce to a simmer, and let the soup cook for about 45 minutes.

3. Stir in the mustard, vinegar, cream, salt, and pepper, and cook for another 12 minutes.

4. Stir in the spinach leaves, and let cook for another 5 minutes.

5. Serve in soup bowls, topped with a dollop of marinara sauce and Parmesan cheese.

Perfect Posole

This posole is incredible — I liken it to a thick and creamy tortilla soup, but better! Serve it with an array of toppings (suggestions are listed below), and let your guests go to town gussying it up. This hominy-heavy recipe is vegetarian, and I like it that way. If you want to throw in some pork shoulder, go for it, but I'm not sure it needs it (though I have been known to prepare it the day after Thanksgiving with leftover turkey). Whichever way you choose, you can't go wrong.

- ☐ 2 T. vegetable oil
- ☐ 8 cloves garlic, chopped
- ☐ 3 white onions, chopped
- ☐ 2 T. cumin
- ☐ 1 T. chili powder
- ☐ 4 cups stock (vegetable or chicken)
- ☐ 6 T. masa harina, a highly ground cornmeal
- ☐ 1 T. brown sugar
- ☐ 1 T. cold water
- ☐ 1 16-oz. can white hominy
- ☐ 1 8-oz. can pinto beans, drained
- ☐ 1 T. kosher salt
- ☐ 1 T. ground black pepper

Suggested toppings: Cut limes, sour cream, black olives, grated Monterey Jack cheese, sliced jalapeno peppers, chopped cilantro, hot sauce.

Perfect Posole *(Continued)*

1. Heat the oil in a large soup pot over medium-high heat. Once heated, sauté the garlic and onions for about 4 minutes, or until softened. Stir in the cumin and chili powder, and cook for a few minutes more.

2. Stir in the stock and simmer another 5 minutes.

3. In a small bowl, mix together the masa harina, sugar, and water, until smooth. Add this mixture to the stock, stirring well.

4. Bring the soup to a boil and then reduce the heat to low, cover, and simmer for about 15 minutes.

5. Add the hominy and beans, and combine well.

6. Cover again and simmer on low for another 30 minutes.

7. Season with salt and pepper. Puree ½ of the mixture in a food processor or blender, then return to the pot, stirring well.

8. Serve in bowls with a variety of toppings (see the suggestions below the ingredients list), allowing your guests to gussy up and top the soup however they like.

Indian-Inspired Beef and Lentil Chili

I know I included a more standard chili recipe, and also a more traditional lentil soup recipe. But I love this mash-up of the two, with just the right addition of Indian cuisine embellishments. If you haven't noticed, I gravitate to thicker soups — and this is such a unique, thick, and super-yummy addition to your soup game.

- ☐ 1 T. olive oil
- ☐ 1 white onion, diced
- ☐ 4 t. finely chopped ginger
- ☐ ½ T. curry powder
- ☐ ½ T. garam masala
- ☐ 1 lb. ground beef
- ☐ 1 c. dried lentils, rinsed
- ☐ ¼ c. tomato paste
- ☐ 3 ½ c. water
- ☐ 1 13.5-oz. can coconut milk
- ☐ ½ c. finely chopped fresh cilantro
- ☐ 2 T. fresh lemon juice
- ☐ Plain yogurt, for serving

Indian-Inspired Beef and Lentil Chili *(Continued)*

1. In a large soup pot, heat the oil over medium heat. Add the onion and cook for about 9 minutes, or until softened, stirring often.

2. Add the ginger, curry powder, and garam masala, and cook for an additional 2 minutes.

3. Add in the ground beef and cook until browned, about 5 minutes, breaking up the beef as you stir.

4. Stir in the lentils and the tomato paste. Cook, stirring, for 1 minute, and then add the water, coconut milk, and cilantro. Bring to a simmer, and cook for about 25 minutes, or until the lentils are softened.

5. Remove from the heat and stir in the lemon juice. Serve in bowls, with a dollop of yogurt on top, and additional cilantro garnish if desired.

Groovalicious Greek Lemon Soup

5

One of my best friends throughout middle school, high school, and college is the uber-Greek, Nick Manolopoulos. During high school, I used to love to hang out at his house and watch his mom, Betty, cook various Greek delicacies — and this Greek lemon soup was my favorite. I've been making this version of her recipe since then — it's so fresh and vibrant and lemony and a long-time staple of mine.

- ☐ 3 T. olive oil
- ☐ 2 c. chopped mirepoix (²/₃ c. each white onions, carrots, celery)
- ☐ ½ t. kosher salt
- ☐ ½ t. ground black pepper
- ☐ 1 c. farro
- ☐ 4 c. chicken broth
- ☐ 3 c. water
- ☐ 1 T. lemon zest
- ☐ 1 c. shredded cooked chicken
- ☐ 3 T. fresh lemon juice
- ☐ 3 eggs
- ☐ 2 T. chopped fresh dill

Groovalicious Greek Lemon Soup *(Continued)*

1. Heat the oil in a large soup pot over medium-high heat.

2. Add the mirepoix, salt, and pepper. Cook, stirring occasionally, until the vegetables soften up, about 5 minutes.

3. Add the farro, and cook until toasted, stirring the whole time, about 2 minutes.

4. Add the broth and water, cover, and bring to a boil.

5. Add the lemon zest, reduce the heat to medium-low, and simmer until the farro is tender, about 15 minutes.

6. Add the chicken and stir.

7. In a separate small bowl, whisk together the lemon juice and eggs. Stir in ½ cup of the hot soup broth, whisking constantly. Slowly stir the hot egg mixture into the soup.

8. Cook the soup over medium-low heat, stirring constantly, until thickened, about 4 minutes. Season with another ¼ t. salt.

9. Serve in soup bowls, sprinkled with the chopped dill and a little bit of black pepper.

Tip-Top
Two-Pumpkin Soup

Those who know me well know that I love pumpkin in everything — from pumpkin spice lattes to pumpkin cookies (see the Desserts chapter!) to roasted pumpkin to all forms of pumpkin dessert — I can't get enough! And, making this unique variation of pumpkin soup is so fulfilling and easy. By the way, you can make the first part of this recipe (Step 1 below), and then add literally any vegetable to Step 2, and it's delicious. I also use this recipe for a great mixed mushroom soup, zucchini soup (add a bit of mint instead of juniper berries), and really any substitution you want to make. It's so good! I used canned pumpkin here — it's the easiest way — but I also use a fresh pumpkin cut into cubes if I have more time. It's thick, comforting, and soooooo tasty.

- [ ] 1 lb. butter
- [ ] 2 leeks, chopped, whites only
- [ ] 2 white onions, chopped
- [ ] 4 shallots, chopped
- [ ] 2 lbs. chopped butternut squash
- [ ] 2 15-oz cans pumpkin
- [ ] 6 c. vegetable stock
- [ ] 2 t. ground juniper berries
- [ ] Kosher salt
- [ ] Croutons, for garnish

Tip-Top Two-Pumpkin Soup *(Continued)*

1. In a large soup pot, melt the butter over medium heat. Add the leeks, onions, and shallots, and cook until well softened, about 10 minutes.

2. Add the chopped squash, stir well, and cook for another 4 minutes. Stir in the canned pumpkin and stock.

3. Bring to a boil, and then reduce the heat to low and simmer until the squash is softened, about 20 minutes.

4. Stir in the ground juniper berries.

5. Working in batches, transfer the soup to a blender and mix well.

6. Once the soup is all blended, season with salt to taste.

7. Serve with croutons.

Moroccan Meatball Soup

SERVES
4

The Mulligans are a meatball-lovin' family. We adore versions made from turkey, pork, beef, or with plant-based ingredients — you name it — and we make them a lot. Sure, I cheat sometimes and use frozen, but they are fun and easy to make from scratch. Why not throw them into a soup with a bunch of veggies and couscous, and invite some Moroccan spices to the party? This soup is bursting with flavor and works great as an entrée or a starter/accompaniment.

- ☐ 1 c. chopped fresh cilantro
- ☐ 1 bunch green onions, chopped
- ☐ 1 lb. ground beef
- ☐ 1 egg, lightly beaten
- ☐ 2 T. harissa
- ☐ 1 ½ t. cumin
- ☐ ½ t. kosher salt
- ☐ 2 T. olive oil
- ☐ 4 carrots, cut into small slices
- ☐ 4 c. chicken (or vegetable) broth
- ☐ 2 c. water
- ☐ ½ c. whole wheat couscous
- ☐ 10 oz. kale leaves, chopped

Morrocan Meatball Soup *(Continued)*

1. In a food processor, pulse the cilantro and green onions well.

2. In a large mixing bowl, combine ½ of the cilantro mixture, ground beef, beaten egg, 1 tablespoon of harissa, ½ teaspoon of cumin, and salt. Using your hands, form 20 golf ball-sized meatballs and set aside.

3. In a large soup pot, heat the oil over medium heat. Add the carrots and cook for about 5 minutes, stirring occasionally, until they start to brown. Add the remaining cilantro mixture, 1 tablespoon of harissa, and 1 teaspoon of cumin, and cook for 1 minute, stirring constantly.

4. Add the broth and water, and bring to a simmer. Cook for about 3 minutes.

5. Gently drop the meatballs into the simmering soup and cook for about 7 minutes.

6. Add the couscous and kale leaves and cook for about 5 minutes, or until the couscous is soft.

7. Season with salt to taste and serve with additional cilantro leaves sprinkled on top.

Slow Cooker Chicken Chili

8
SERVES
6-8

I wrestled with this one. I knew I wanted to add a chili recipe, and I've got dozens of them that I cycle through constantly. After much deliberation, I think this one is the real keeper — the sweet potatoes are a great secret ingredient, and the random array of spices (yes, including tapioca pudding mix) give this easy chili a very distinctive and pleasing punch. And you know I love my slow cooker. Dump it all in and go.

- ☐ 2 lbs. ground chicken
- ☐ 3 T. chili powder
- ☐ 1 15-oz. can white beans, drained and rinsed
- ☐ 1 15-oz. can kidney beans, drained and rinsed
- ☐ 2 28-oz. cans fire-roasted diced tomatoes
- ☐ 16 oz. chicken broth
- ☐ 1 medium sweet potato, peeled and shredded

- ☐ ¼ c. instant tapioca mix
- ☐ 2 T. soy sauce
- ☐ 1 T. kosher salt
- ☐ 1 T. onion powder
- ☐ 2 t. garlic powder
- ☐ 1 t. dried oregano
- ☐ 1 t. cumin
- ☐ ½ t. cinnamon
- ☐ Pinch of ground cloves
- ☐ ½ c. lager beer

Slow Cooker Chicken Chili *(Continued)*

Suggested toppings: shredded cheese, sour cream, black olives, chopped jalapeno peppers

1. Place all ingredients into a slow cooker and stir well.

2. Cover and cook on the low setting for 6 hours.

3. Before serving, taste and season if needed with an additional teaspoon chili powder and salt and pepper. Serve with whatever optional toppings you desire!

Perfect 10 Chorizo Stew

9

SERVES
4

This is a unique soup that my family gulps down. The chorizo and paprika give it a smoky and very acute taste. You can go two ways with the chorizo: either add sliced chorizo sausage, which results in a more traditional stew, or go with tubes of minced chorizo to create a brothier soup (pictured). This is one soup that will impress your guests and have them begging for the recipe.

☐ 3 T. olive oil

☐ 1 white onion, chopped

☐ 1 t. kosher salt

☐ 3 9-oz. tubes chorizo (or 3 8-oz. fully cooked chorizo sausages)

☐ 3 cloves garlic, minced

☐ 3 russet potatoes, peeled and cut into 1-in. chunks

☐ ½ t. ground black pepper

☐ 4 c. chicken broth

☐ 2 bay leaves

☐ 1 t. smoked paprika

☐ 1 bunch rainbow chard leaves, stems removed and chopped

☐ Crusty bread, for dipping

Perfect 10 Chorizo Stew *(Continued)*

1. Heat the oil in a large soup pot over medium-high heat. Add the onion, season with ½ teaspoon of the salt, and cook until soft and starting to brown, about 5 minutes.

2. Add the chorizo and cook, stirring occasionally, until the chorizo starts to brown, about 5 minutes.

3. Stir in the garlic and cook for 1 minute, stirring well. Add the potatoes, another ½ teaspoon of salt, and the pepper. Cook until mixed well, about 3 minutes.

4. Add the broth, bay leaves, and smoked paprika, and bring to a simmer. Cover, reduce the heat to medium, and simmer for about 15 minutes.

5. Add the chard, cover, and cook until the potatoes are tender, about 3 minutes.

6. Season to taste with salt and pepper.

7. Serve in bowls alongside some crusty bread for dipping.

Good Old-Fashioned Chicken Veggie Rice Soup

10 SERVES 4-6

I know I already have a recipe for a lemony chicken soup, but I couldn't resist adding a family favorite — good old-fashioned chicken veggie rice soup. This recipe is awesome. You can, of course, throw in any other combinations of herbs and veggies, but I like this version best, which I've honed over the years. (Don't skimp on the Parmesan rind — it's a great addition to many soups I make.) Pour yourself a big mug full of this savory delight and cozy up to the fire!

- ☐ 2 T. olive oil
- ☐ 1½ c. diced mirepoix (½ c. each white onions, carrots, celery)
- ☐ ½ c. English peas
- ☐ 2 c. chicken stock
- ☐ 3 c. vegetable stock
- ☐ 1 Parmesan cheese rind
- ☐ 1 t. kosher salt
- ☐ 2 c. shredded (or chopped) cooked chicken
- ☐ 1 c. cooked brown rice
- ☐ 1 pinch turmeric
- ☐ ¼ c. chopped fresh thyme

Good Old-Fashioned Chicken Veggie Rice Soup *(Continued)*

1. Heat the oil over medium heat in large soup pot. Add in the vegetables and cook until soft, about 5 minutes.

2. Stir in both broths, the Parmesan rind, and salt, and bring to a boil. Reduce the heat to low, and let the soup simmer for at least 10 minutes.

3. Stir in the chicken, rice, turmeric, and thyme, and simmer for an additional 5 minutes. Remove the Parmesan rind when done cooking.

4. Serve hot!

ENTRÉES

Oh no! You've been assigned the dreaded main course. Now what? With a list like this, you should feel confident raising your hand and volunteering to bring an entrée or planning a dinner party or birthday event. Whatever the mission, any one of these Tim's Top Ten entrées should be guaranteed to fit the bill. I've tried to include something from all main categories — including seafood, poultry, pizza, comfort food, a few internationally themed dishes, and vegetarian. All ten recipes are tried and true, and all ten are sure to be crowd-pleasers.

Slammin' Soy Glazed Salmon

SERVES
4

Oh, how my family loves salmon! It's something I make for people all the time, particularly at barbecues and on outdoor-dining nights. However, when barbecuing is not in the cards, roasting salmon is so easy and quick. This recipe is one I've been cooking since college and making a few tweaks to along the way. I think the hot honey is a great addition. This salmon is addictive, and a winner!

- ☐ 1 T. hot honey
- ☐ 2 ½ t. soy sauce
- ☐ ½ t. cornstarch
- ☐ 4 salmon filets
- ☐ ½ t. sesame oil
- ☐ Kosher salt
- ☐ Sesame seeds and lemon slices, for garnish

1. Preheat the oven to 400 degrees.

2. In a small microwave-safe bowl, combine the honey, soy sauce, and cornstarch and microwave for 30 seconds, or until the marinade is simmering.

3. Rub the sesame oil over the salmon filets and season lightly with salt.

4. Place the filets in a baking dish and bake for 6 minutes.

5. Remove the filets from the oven, and brush the marinade over the filets. Return the filets to the oven and cook for 8 to 10 minutes, or until the salmon is cooked to your liking. (I like mine cooked through.)

6. Serve with a sprinkling of sesame seeds and lemon slices over the top.

Tim's Tostadas

I would be remiss in not adding a Mexican entrée here considering I cook Mexican food for my family multiple times a week. This is such an easy way to cook tostadas without frying! And, making your own refried beans is so easy and they are so much better than canned ones. Also, with the basic foundation of the baked tostada shell and the refried beans, you can create a mini-masterpiece with whatever toppings you choose! I promise, once you make your own tostadas, you'll commit to this recipe (or some creative variation) every time. Enjoy!

- ☐ 6 small yellow corn tortillas
- ☐ Canola oil
- ☐ Kosher salt
- ☐ ¼ c. coconut oil
- ☐ ½ white onion, chopped
- ☐ 2 T. minced garlic
- ☐ 1 t. cumin
- ☐ ½ t. coriander
- ☐ 2 15.5-oz. cans pinto beans, drained and rinsed
- ☐ 1 c. chicken stock

- ☐ 1 T. fresh lime juice
- ☐ 2 T. vegetable oil
- ☐ ½ red onion, chopped
- ☐ 1 lb. ground beef (or substitute turkey or plant-based meat)
- ☐ 2 T. tomato paste
- ☐ 1 T. chili powder
- ☐ 1 ½ c. shredded Monterey Jack cheese
- ☐ ½ c. sour cream
- ☐ Shredded lettuce and chopped cilantro, for garnish

Tim's Tostadas *(Continued)*

Prepare the tostada base:

1. Preheat the oven to 350 degrees.

2. Brush both sides of the tortillas with canola oil.

3. Place the tortillas on a baking sheet and sprinkle with salt.

4. Bake until crispy, about 18 to 20 minutes. Let cool.

Prepare the refried beans:

1. Heat the coconut oil in a cast-iron skillet over medium heat.

2. Add the diced white onion and cook until softened, about 3 to 4 minutes.

3. Stir in 1 tablespoon of the garlic, cumin, coriander, and ½ teaspoon salt, and cook for 1 minute.

4. Add the beans and chicken stock and bring to a boil.

5. Cook until the stock has reduced by half and the mixture has thickened up, about 6 minutes.

6. Remove from the heat and mash up the beans the best you can with a large spoon or a potato masher. If you need to thin them, add a little stock to get a thick but stirrable consistency.

7. Stir in the lime juice and add a pinch of salt.

Prepare the beef topping:

1. Heat the vegetable oil in a large skillet over medium-high heat.

2. Add the chopped red onion and cook for about 5 minutes, or until soft.

3. Add the remaining 1 tablespoon of garlic and cook for 1 minute.

4. Add the beef and ½ teaspoon salt and cook until browned, about 3 to 4 minutes.

5. Add the tomato paste and chili powder, and cook for another 2 minutes.

Put it all together:

1. Spread a layer of refried beans on the tostadas.

2. Top with a layer of the beef and sprinkle the cheese on top.

3. Thin the sour cream in a small bowl with 2 tablespoons water.

4. Drizzle with the sour cream and then top with shredded lettuce and cilantro.

Baked Chicken with Lemon and Olives

How could I have a Top Ten list of entrées and not include a chicken dish? I included this one because it's easy and will have everybody asking you for the recipe. In fact, this is a variation of a dish I used to cook with my mom — the lemons and green olives mixed with the honey and cumin make for a perfect Mediterranean-themed entrée. And just look how pretty it is!

- ☐ ¼ c. fresh lemon juice
- ☐ ¼ c. orange juice
- ☐ 3 T. olive oil
- ☐ 2 T. honey
- ☐ ¾ t. cumin
- ☐ 6 cloves garlic, chopped
- ☐ 4 boneless chicken breasts
- ☐ ½ t. kosher salt
- ☐ ½ t. ground black pepper
- ☐ 1 c. pitted green olives, cut in half (can use pimento-stuffed as well)
- ☐ 1 lemon, cut into thin slices
- ☐ ¼ c. chopped fresh Italian parsley

Baked Chicken with Lemon and Olives *(Continued)*

1. Preheat the oven to 400 degrees.

2. In a medium mixing bowl, combine the juices, oil, honey, cumin, and garlic.

3. Stir in the chicken breasts, and and let them marinate in the refrigerator for 30 minutes.

4. Remove the chicken breasts from the marinade and set aside.

5. Pour the marinade in a 9 x 9-inch baking dish.

6. Heat a large skillet over medium-high heat and add the chicken breasts. Cook for 3 minutes on each side, ensuring both sides are browned well.

7. Place the chicken breasts in the baking dish and season with the salt and pepper.

8. Top the chicken with the olives and lemon slices.

9. Bake for 40 minutes, or until the chicken reaches 165 degrees.

10. Remove the chicken from the baking dish, reserving the liquids. Pour the liquids into a saucepan. Bring to a boil, and cook for about 3 minutes, or until the sauce thickens a bit. Stir in the olives.

11. Spoon the sauce over the chicken on a serving platter, and top with the lemons and parsley.

Transcendent Turkey Spinach Bowls

I love serving my family "bowl" dinners — some sort of starch piled with veggies and protein with a good drizzle of sauce of some sort. I've got dozens of these bowl dinners in my rotating recipe repertoire. I think bowls are also a good way to cook something fun, easy, and healthy! And the mixture of turkey and spinach, with curry and spices, is delectable. This is a great recipe for a casual family dinner, a dinner for one, or to make the night before and bring to work for lunch the next day.

- ☐ 1 large white onion, chopped

- ☐ 3 cloves garlic, minced

- ☐ ¼ c. chopped fresh ginger

- ☐ 1 T. curry powder

- ☐ Kosher salt

- ☐ 1 c. plain yogurt

- ☐ 2 T. vegetable oil

- ☐ 1 lb. ground turkey (or substitute tofu crumbles)

- ☐ 1 c. garbanzo beans

- ☐ 1 10-oz. package frozen chopped spinach, thawed and squeezed dry

- ☐ ¼ c. chopped cilantro

- ☐ 3 c. cooked brown rice

- ☐ Chopped cilantro, for garnish

Transcendent Turkey Spinach Bowls *(Continued)*

1. Puree ½ of the onion, garlic, ginger, curry powder, 2 tablespoons water, and ½ teaspoon salt in a food processor until smooth; set aside.

2. Mix the yogurt with ¼ cup water and set aside.

3. Heat the oil in a large skillet over high heat.

4. Add the remaining onion and cook, stirring often, until the onion is lightly browned and softened, about 3 to 4 minutes.

5. Add the turkey and garbanzo beans and cook until the meat is lightly browned, about 3 minutes.

6. Add the onion-spice mixture to the skillet and cook, stirring occasionally, for 4 minutes.

7. Reduce the heat to low and stir in the spinach and ¾ cup of the yogurt. Cook, stirring, for 3 to 4 minutes.

8. Stir in the cilantro and ¼ teaspoon of salt.

9. Divide the rice among 4 serving bowls and spoon the turkey mixture over the rice. Top each bowl with a drizzle of the remaining yogurt along with additional chopped cilantro for garnish.

Judy's Amped-Up Tuna Casserole

SERVES
6-8

When putting my recipe lists together for this book, I really tried to include recipes from my own relatives. I wish I could say I had a whole box of recipes from my mother, Judy, but that's not the case. She did like to cook, and we spent many, many hours cooking together, particularly during the holidays. However, if I had to come up with one weeknight dinner that was a standby in our house, it would have to be my mother's tuna casserole, which she always "zhuzhed up" with her secret ingredient…Cheez-It® crackers! I've been making this over the years in homage to my mother, Judy, and have "modernized" it somewhat. (No more canned cream of mushroom soup!) It's fun, harkens to one's childhood, and is very addictive. Thanks, Mom!!

- ☐ 6 T. butter
- ☐ 1 lb. white mushrooms, sliced
- ☐ 2 shallots, diced
- ☐ 1 celery stalk, finely chopped
- ☐ 3 cloves garlic, chopped
- ☐ Kosher salt
- ☐ Ground black pepper
- ☐ ¼ c. flour
- ☐ ⅓ c. dry sherry
- ☐ 1 c. chicken stock
- ☐ 1 c. milk
- ☐ 1 12-oz. bag wide egg noodles
- ☐ ¼ c. chopped fresh dill
- ☐ ½ c. chopped fresh parsley
- ☐ ½ c. sour cream
- ☐ 1 T. Dijon mustard
- ☐ ½ c. frozen lima beans
- ☐ 2 cans tuna, drained
- ☐ 1 ½ c. Cheez-It® crackers (I like the spicy hot ones!)
- ☐ 1 c. grated Parmigiano-Reggiano cheese
- ☐ ¼ c. chopped cornichons

Judy's Amped-Up Tuna Casserole *(Continued)*

1. In a large skillet, melt the butter over medium-high heat. Add the mushrooms and cook, stirring, for about 6 minutes, or until browned. Reduce the heat and add the shallots, celery, and garlic. Season with salt and pepper. Cook, stirring, for about 4 minutes, or until the vegetables are softened.

2. Add the flour and stir to ensure the vegetables are coated. Add the sherry and cook for 1 minute. Whisk in the stock and bring to a boil.

3. Add the milk and cook for about 4 minutes, or until the sauce is thickened and reduced by about one third.

4. Cook the noodles in salted boiling water for 5 minutes. Drain the noodles, but reserve ½ cup of the pasta water.

5. Add the dill, ¼ cup of the parsley, sour cream, and mustard to the skillet. Stir in the lima beans and cook for about 1 minute. Now fold in the tuna.

6. Stir in the noodles, ensuring they are fully coated with the sauce. Add the reserved cooking water to make a nice saucy dish and pour the sauce into a casserole dish (3 quart is best).

7. In a large freezer bag, crush the Cheez-It® crackers. Add the cheese to the bag and shake to combine. Scatter the cheese-cracker mixture over the dish.

8. Place the dish under a broiler for a few minutes, or until the topping is browned and the casserole is bubbling around the edges.

9. Prior to serving, scatter the top with the remaining parsley and the cornichons.

Pass the Pasticcio

My favorite place in the world is Greece. Specifically, the Greek islands. I spent two crazy weeks in law school sleeping on the beach in Mykonos with my good friend Theresa, and then I went back with a group of friends to the exact same beach for my fiftieth birthday. Besides the beautiful scenery and beaches, it's the food I crave. Growing up, my best friend in high school was Greek, and his mother would make the yummiest food I'd ever had including a Greek lemon soup (see the recipe on p. 99) and pasticcio, a savory baked pasta dish that I am delighted to share with you here. I've been making this regularly since those memorable days long ago. It's decadent, spiced with nutmeg and cinnamon. (I amp it up a bit with pumpkin pie spice.) So good!

☐ 4 T. olive oil

☐ 1 large white onion, chopped

☐ 3 T. chopped fresh parsley

☐ 3 cloves garlic, chopped

☐ 1 lb. ground beef

☐ 1 lb. ground pork

☐ ½ t. kosher salt

☐ ½ t. ground black pepper

☐ 1 t. pumpkin pie spice

☐ ½ c. white wine

☐ 1 14-oz. can chopped tomatoes

☐ 1 16-oz. package penne pasta

☐ 3 T. butter

☐ 1 t. dried mint

☐ 2 T. breadcrumbs

Bechamel Sauce

☐ 8 T. (1 stick) butter

☐ 1 c. flour

☐ 4 c. milk

☐ 1 t. nutmeg

☐ Kosher salt

☐ Ground black pepper

Pass the Pasticcio *(Continued)*

1. Preheat the oven to 350 degrees.

2. Heat the oil in a large saucepan and sauté the onion until it starts to brown, about 3 minutes. Stir in the parsley and garlic, and let the ingredients incorporate for about 1 minute.

3. Stir in both ground meats, breaking them up to incorporate well with the onions. Once the meat starts to brown, season with salt, pepper, and the pumpkin pie spice.

4. Add the wine and let cook until the liquid evaporates. Stir in the tomatoes, along with a ½ cup of water, and cook over medium heat until the tomatoes are cooked, about 15 minutes. Remove from the heat.

5. While the tomato mixture is cooking, cook the penne in boiling salted water. Cook for a few minutes less than the directions call for on the box. (They should be slightly al dente.) Drain the noodles and set them aside in a large bowl.

6. Mix the butter and mint into the hot noodles, making sure the butter completely melts.

7. Pour half of the buttery noodles into a casserole or baking dish. Add the meat mixture, making sure the lower layer of noodles is completely covered. Cover the meat layer with the remaining noodles. Set aside.

8. Prepare the bechamel sauce: Melt the butter in a saucepan. Once melted, whisk in the flour and cook for a few minutes, stirring constantly. Slowly whisk in the milk.

Pass the Pasticcio *(Continued)*

9. Once the sauce has a smooth consistency, season it well with a pinch of the salt, a pinch of the pepper, and nutmeg. Continue to cook, stirring frequently, for about 5 minutes. By now, you should have a smooth, thick sauce. Taste and season with more salt, pepper, and nutmeg as needed. It should not be bland.

10. Pour the sauce over the pasta dish, spreading it evenly over the top. Sprinkle with the breadcrumbs, and then bake for about 40 minutes, or until the top is nicely golden-brown in spots.

11. Remove the dish from the oven and let it cool slightly before serving to firm it up a bit. Cut into squares and serve!

Emiel's Cheeseburger Lasagn-YAY!

So...I've seen various versions of hamburger casserole, cheeseburger casserole, lasagna, and "tray bakes" floating around, and I have tried most of them. Why? My family loves casseroles! This dish, which I think is just about perfect, is the staple in our house for birthday dinners. It's decadent, old school, and soooooo good. It's a cheeseburger in a lasagna form like you've never had before.

Beef Layer

- ☐ 8 strips bacon, chopped
- ☐ 1 T. olive oil
- ☐ 2 lbs. ground beef
- ☐ 2 t. onion powder
- ☐ 2 t. garlic powder
- ☐ 2 t. dried oregano
- ☐ 2 t. kosher salt
- ☐ 1 t. ground black pepper

Sauce Layer

- ☐ 1 T. butter
- ☐ 1 T. flour
- ☐ 2 c. milk
- ☐ 2 c. heavy cream
- ☐ 2 T. Dijon mustard
- ☐ Kosher salt

Remaining Layers

- ☐ 2 lb. frozen cheese pirogis or ravioli
- ☐ 8 slices Swiss cheese
- ☐ 8 slices American cheese
- ☐ 2 Roma tomatoes, diced
- ☐ 8 oz. shredded Cheddar and Monterrey Jack cheese blend
- ☐ 1 head iceberg lettuce, finely shredded
- ☐ ¼ c. very thinly sliced red onions
- ☐ 2 T. dill pickle brine

Emiel's Cheeseburger Lasagn-YAY! *(Continued)*

1. Prepare the meat: In a large skillet, cook the bacon pieces on medium heat. Stir until crisp, then remove the bacon from the pan with a slotted spoon onto a paper towel–lined plate, reserving the drippings in the pan.

2. Add the oil, beef, onion and garlic powders, oregano, salt, and pepper to the skillet. Cook the beef until browned, breaking it into bits and stirring well. Remove the beef with a slotted spoon to a bowl, leaving the drippings in the pan for the sauce.

3. Prepare the mustard sauce: Add the butter and flour to the warmed skillet. Cook, whisking constantly, for a few minutes. Slowly whisk in the milk. Once it starts to thicken, add the heavy cream and continue to cook until the sauce thickens again. Add the mustard and stir — the sauce should be velvety thick. Season with a pinch of salt.

4. Prepare the casserole: Preheat the oven to 350 degrees. In a 9 x 13-inch dish, layer the casserole. Start with a few heaping spoonfuls of the sauce. Add half of the frozen pierogi or ravioli, then the Swiss cheese slices, followed by half of the seasoned meat, half of the tomatoes, and half of the sauce. Top that with the remaining frozen pierogi or ravioli, then the American cheese slices, then the remaining beef, remaining tomatoes, remaining sauce, and then the bacon pieces. Top with the cheese blend.

5. Bake until bubbly and browned on top, about 35 minutes.

6. Toss the iceberg lettuce and red onion in a small bowl with the pickle brine. Present each casserole serving with the lettuce on the top.

Foolproof Fideo with Spicy Tomato Sauce

One of my best longtime friends (since eighth grade!) is Rachael. Her mother, Lupe, whipped up many an authentic Mexican meal for me all through high school, college, and still to this day. I literally crave her homemade Mexican rice and beans, cheese and onion enchiladas, and salsa, but it's her fideo that always blows me away. This is not exactly her recipe, but my own re-creation. It's so comforting — like a Mexican spiced spaghetti. Yum!

☐ 16 oz. spaghetti, broken up into small pieces

☐ 2 T. olive oil

☐ 1 ½ c. chopped green onions

☐ 4 t. cumin

☐ 3 c. chicken broth

☐ 2 14-oz. cans diced tomatoes with chilies

☐ Kosher salt

☐ Chopped fresh cilantro, for garnish

☐ Cotija or queso fresco cheese crumbles, for garnish

1. Add the spaghetti and oil to a skillet and toast, stirring constantly, over low heat until the noodles start to brown, about 5 minutes.

2. Add the green onions and cumin and mix well.

3. Add the broth and diced tomatoes, turn up the heat to medium, and simmer until the spaghetti softens, about 14 minutes. (I like it slightly al dente.)

4. Season with salt to taste.

5. Serve topped with the chopped cilantro and the crumbled cheese. Enjoy!

Swedish Meatball Marsala Mashup

I've mentioned that my mother was not a bang-up cook, but the dishes I fondly recall from my childhood are various incarnations of classic comfort foods such as Swedish meatballs, goulash, stroganoff, and Marsala sauce dishes. I tried to combine much of these dishes into a mashup of comfort classics—and this recipe has proven to be a staple for work parties. Get copies of the recipe ready for your coworkers.

- ☐ 1 lb. ground beef
- ☐ ½ c. panko breadcrumbs
- ☐ ½ white onion, chopped (about ¾ c.)
- ☐ ½ t. garlic powder
- ☐ 1 egg
- ☐ Kosher salt
- ☐ Ground black pepper
- ☐ 2 T. vegetable oil
- ☐ 1 ½ c. beef broth
- ☐ 2 c. milk
- ☐ ½ c. Marsala wine
- ☐ 1 T. Worcestershire sauce
- ☐ 4 c. uncooked egg noodles
- ☐ ½ c. chopped parsley
- ☐ 1 c. grated Parmesan cheese

Sweedish Meatball Marsala Mashup *(Continued)*

1. In a large mixing bowl, combine the beef, breadcrumbs, onion, garlic powder, egg, and ½ tablespoon each of salt and pepper. Using your hands, mix the ingredients until well combined and form small ping-pong-ball-sized meatballs. (You should be able to make 12 to 16 of these.)

2. Heat the oil in a large pot over medium-high heat. Place the meatballs into the pot and cook for about 1 minute. Flip each meatball over.

3. Add the broth, milk, wine, ½ tablespoon each of salt and pepper, and the Worcestershire sauce, and stir well.

4. Bring to a boil, and then drop in the egg noodles. Stir constantly until the pasta is cooked and the liquid is reduced to a nice sauce consistency, covering all the noodles well, about 8 minutes.

5. Add the parsley and cheese, stirring well until the cheese melts.

6. Serve!

Jerry's Special Pizza

10

SERVES
2-4

In my hometown of Richland, Washington, there were many a night when dinner at my house consisted of pizza from a local tavern, The Gaslight. One pizza our family always gravitated toward was the Jerry's Special, which was loaded with diced pepperoni and diced dill pickles. Yes, dill pickles! I've grown up now craving dill pickles on my pizza, and recreated my own version to include diced salami and pickles. Of course, you can use store-bought pizza sauce, but this sauce recipe is really good and simple. Alas, I don't make my own dough, but knock yourself out if you want to.

Pizza Sauce

☐ 1 28-oz. can whole peeled tomatoes

☐ 1 T. olive oil

☐ 1 T. unsalted butter

☐ 2 cloves garlic, diced

☐ 1 t. dried oregano

☐ 1 pinch red pepper flakes

☐ Kosher salt

☐ 1 medium yellow onion, cut into quarters

☐ ¼ c. fresh chopped basil

Pizza

☐ Store-bought pizza dough, or cauliflower crusts (pictured below)

☐ Grated mozzarella cheese

☐ Diced dill pickles

☐ Diced salami

☐ Olive oil, for drizzling

☐ Hot honey, for drizzling

Jerry's Special Pizza *(Continued)*

1. Make the sauce: In a food processor or blender, liquefy the tomatoes and their juices until puréed. Set aside.

2. In a medium saucepan, heat the oil and butter until the butter is melted. Add the garlic, oregano, red pepper flakes, and a large pinch of salt and cook, stirring frequently, for about 3 minutes.

3. Add the puréed tomatoes, onion, and basil. Bring to a simmer, and then reduce the heat to low and cook, stirring occasionally, until the sauce is reduced by half, about 1 hour. Discard the onions and basil. Season to taste with salt.

4. Assemble the pizza: Preheat the oven to 425 degrees.

5. Either roll the dough into your preferred size and shape of pizza, or place your store-bought crusts on a pizza pan or cookie sheet. Spread with a full layer of the sauce.

6. Top with mozzarella, and then scatter the top with the pickles and salami. Drizzle olive oil over the top.

7. Bake for 10 to 12 minutes, or until the cheese is bubbling and the crust is done.

8. Before serving, drizzle hot honey over the top. Yum!

DESSERTS

I'm a dessert junkie. I could give up any food except for cakes, cookies, puddings … you name it. I've been whipping up desserts for my family and friends for as long as I can remember. I want to be very transparent here — I'm not a "baker." Admittedly, I am not good at yeast-based desserts. I'm more like a 1950s or 1960s housewife when it comes to dessert preferences, preferring the old classics that I can update in my own way. Most of these recipes are desserts that go back to my youth, and I've probably made them hundreds of times. I can't even guess how many people have begged me for my Pumpkin Cookies, or Wyoming Whoppers, or Banana Cream Pie recipes. I have to thank my aunts and neighbors over the years who provided me with the initial recipes here, which I've either kept intact or adjusted slightly. I hope you enjoy these as much as my waistline has.

Aunt Linda's Wyoming Whopper Cookies

My amazing Aunt Linda proclaims that she can't cook, but two of my favorite recipes of all time are in the book: these awesome cookies and her Hot Peanut Sesame Dip (see the recipe on p. 43). I remember when she made these for me to take on a hike when I was in grade school. They obviously made an impact because I've been making these cookies regularly for the past 40 years. No matter where they are served, everyone wants the recipe. So, courtesy of Aunt Linda, here you go!

- ☐ ⅔ c. unsalted butter, softened
- ☐ 1 ¼ c. light brown sugar
- ☐ ¾ c. sugar
- ☐ 3 beaten eggs
- ☐ 2 t. baking soda
- ☐ 1 ½ c. chunky peanut butter
- ☐ 6 c. old-fashioned oats
- ☐ ½ c. chocolate chips
- ☐ ½ c. butterscotch chips

1. Preheat the oven to 350 degrees.

2. Mix together the butter, sugars, eggs, and baking soda.

3. Stir in the peanut butter, and mix well.

4. Add the oats and combine to form a nicely mixed cookie dough.

5. Add the chips and stir well.

6. Drop by spoonfuls onto greased cookie sheets and bake for 11 minutes, or until soft and very lightly browned.

Aunt Pat's Mokka Balls

SERVES
6 Tostadas

A favorite childhood memory of mine is going to my cousins', the Cassidys', house every Christmas. The house was always decorated to the nines, and there would be a huge spread of Aunt Pat's delectable baked goods. While there are several favorites I've been making over the years, trying to keep her traditions alive, I think this recipe is the best. It's so stupidly basic — homemade angel food cake cut in small squares, frosted, and rolled in salty chopped peanuts. How can something so basic be so amazing? The assembly line process is messy, but that's part of the fun. And don't ask me what the name means — I have no clue.

Angel Food Cake

☐ 4 eggs

☐ 2 c. sugar

☐ 2 c. flour

☐ 2 t. baking powder

☐ ¼ t. salt

☐ 1 c. milk

☐ ¼ c. unsalted butter, melted

☐ 1 t. vanilla

Icing

☐ 3 c. powdered sugar

☐ ½ c. butter, softened

☐ 3 T. milk

☐ 1 t. vanilla

☐ ¼ t. almond extract

☐ 4 c. chopped salted peanuts

Aunt Pat's Mokka Balls *(Continued)*

1. Preheat the oven to 350 degrees. Spray a 13 x 9-inch baking dish with cooking spray and line with parchment paper, allowing a bit of an overhang over the sides.

2. In a large mixing bowl, beat the eggs with a hand mixer on medium speed for 1 minute. Slowly beat in the sugar and continue beating for 4 minutes.

3. In a separate mixing bowl, combine the flour, baking powder, and salt. Add to the egg mixture, beating on low speed until just incorporated.

4. In a small bowl, beat together the milk, melted butter, and vanilla. Pour the batter into the prepared baking dish.

5. Bake for 40 minutes, or until the cake is golden and springs back when touched. Cool for 15 minutes, then pull it out of the dish using the parchment paper and allow it to cool completely on a wire rack.

6. Prepare the icing: Beat the powdered sugar, softened butter, milk, vanilla, and almond extract, creating a smooth icing.

7. Spread the chopped peanuts on to a plate.

8. Cut the cake into 24 squares. Frost all sides but the bottom of the squares with the icing, then carefully roll in the chopped peanuts. It's messy—use your hands.

9. Refrigerate for at least 1 hour before serving.

Legendary Pumpkin Cookies with Caramel Frosting!

I think this is the recipe that started it all for this cookbook. I've probably had this recipe since I was in the second or third grade, when a neighbor used to make it every Halloween and I got my hands on a copy. Since then, I make these cookies annually for Halloween, and also for my Thanksgiving table. Everybody devours them and wants the recipe. In fact, that interest promoted the spark of an idea to write this cookbook and share all of my favorite time-honored recipes. These cookies are so soft, pumpkin-y, and yummy… and the caramel frosting takes them to another level. I hope they become a part of your traditions as well.

Cookies

- ☐ 2 c. flour
- ☐ ½ t. salt
- ☐ 1 t. baking powder
- ☐ 1 t. baking soda
- ☐ 1 t. cinnamon
- ☐ ½ c. shortening
- ☐ 1 c. sugar
- ☐ 1 c. canned pumpkin
- ☐ 1 egg
- ☐ 1 t. vanilla
- ☐ ½ c. chopped pecans

Caramel Frosting

- ☐ 3 T. butter
- ☐ ¼ c. milk
- ☐ ½ c. brown sugar
- ☐ 1 c. powdered sugar
- ☐ ½ t. vanilla

Legendary Pumpkin Cookies with Caramel Frosting! *(Continued)*

1. Preheat the oven to 350 degrees.

2. In a medium mixing bowl, mix the flour, salt, baking powder, baking soda, and cinnamon well.

3. In a separate bowl, mix the shortening, sugar, pumpkin, egg, and vanilla well. Add the dry ingredients, along with the pecans, and mix to form a dough.

4. Drop by spoonfuls onto a greased cookie sheet and cook for exactly 12 minutes. The cookies should be slightly soft. Let cool before frosting.

5. Make the icing: In a saucepan, bring the butter, milk, and brown sugar to a boil, and then stir constantly for exactly 2 minutes. Remove from the heat and let cool completely.

6. Once cool, stir in the powdered sugar and vanilla — it should be a creamy caramel frosting consistency. Adjust accordingly with powdered sugar or milk, as needed.

7. Frost the cookies and enjoy!

Cherry Pineapple Dump Cake...with Cherry Whip!

I have no idea how dump cakes were created, but to me they may be the greatest culinary invention ever. My own mom, Judy, was not the best cook, but one thing we always craved from her were dump cakes. The title sums it up: dump a bunch of stuff into a baking dish, cover with a package of cake mix and butter, and you're done. Of course, you can make any variation of this — with canned peaches, apple pie filling, blueberry pie filling, and any type of cake mix dumped on top. This particular combo is probably the most classic (is there such a thing as "classic dump cake?") and my favorite. The cherry whipped cream is a great addition.

- ☐ 1 15-oz. can crushed pineapple
- ☐ 1 21-oz. can cherry pie filling
- ☐ 1 box white cake mix
- ☐ 12 T. (1 ½ sticks) unsalted butter
- ☐ Whipped topping (store-bought or homemade)

1. Preheat the oven to 350 degrees.

2. Dump the pineapple and cherry pie filling (reserving a small amount in the can for the whipped cream) into a 13 x 9-inch baking dish and stir together well.

3. Sprinkle the cake mix over the top and spread evenly.

4. Slice the butter into even slices (about ¼-inch thick), and distribute evenly over the top of the mix.

5. Bake until the top is bubbly and lightly browned, about 1 hour.

6. Prepare the whipped topping by stirring in the reserved cherry pie filling.

7. Serve in individual bowls with a dollop of cherry whipped topping on top.

Naughty Banana Cream Pie

Why is this pie naughty? Well, I have to admit that most of my desserts in this chapter lean to the "naughty," but this pie, with its decadent banana-enriched crust; rich, cream-laden custard; and hefty layer of fresh whipped cream on top, is definitely not a diet dish. But it's so good. You can serve it like this and impress, or sometimes for parties I'll make the pie and then scoop it, crust and all, into little party cups for pie-in-a-cup. No matter which way you go, it's a show-stopper.

Custard

- ☐ 5 egg yolks
- ☐ ¼ c. cornstarch
- ☐ 3 c. heavy cream
- ☐ 2 c. sugar
- ☐ 1 t. vanilla

Crust

- ☐ 3 c. graham cracker crumbs
- ☐ ½ c. sugar
- ☐ ½ ripe banana, mashed
- ☐ 8 T. (1 stick) unsalted butter, melted -

Whipped Cream Topping

- ☐ 2 c. heavy cream
- ☐ ½ t. vanilla
- ☐ 2 t. sugar

Pie

- ☐ 3 lb. bananas, sliced into ½-in. slices
- ☐ Caramel sauce for drizzling

Naughty Banana Cream Pie *(Continued)*

Prepare the custard:

1. In a mixing bowl, whisk together the egg yolks, cornstarch, and 1 cup of the heavy cream. Set aside.

2. Combine the remaining 2 cups of heavy cream, sugar, and vanilla in a large saucepan over medium heat. Whisk well, dissolving the sugar and bringing to a boil, for about 10 minutes. Slowly whisk in the egg mixture and whisk constantly until it thickens, about 5 minutes. It will become very thick and break, almost looking curdled. When this happens, remove the custard from the heat and pour into a glass bowl. Cover the bowl with plastic wrap and let the custard cool completely at room temperature.

3. Once cooled, mix the custard with a hand mixer at medium speed to combine fully. The end result should be a thick and creamy yellow custard.

Prepare the crust:

1. Preheat the oven to 350 degrees.

2. In a large mixing bowl, combine the graham cracker crumbs, sugar, and mashed bananas. Add the melted butter and mix well. Press this mixture into a 9-inch pie dish. Bake until lightly browned, about 25 minutes. Let cool completely before assembling the pie.

Assemble the pie:

1. Spread about ½ cup of the custard over the bottom of the pie crust. Layer $1/3$ of the banana slices over the custard, overlapping each other. Spread about 1 cup of the custard over the top of the bananas, and then follow with another $1/3$ of the banana slices. Top with $1/3$ of the custard, and then the remaining banana slices. Cover fully with the remaining custard.

2. Cover the pie with plastic wrap, and refrigerate for at least 4 hours.

Prepare the whipped cream:

1. In a medium size mixing bowl, beat the heavy cream until stiff peaks form. Now stir in the vanilla and sugar, and combine well.

2. When ready to serve, remove the plastic wrap and spread the whipped cream over the top of the pie. Drizzle caramel sauce over the whipped cream. Cut and serve!

Red Velvet Banana Pudding I Could Eat All Day

Who doesn't love pudding cups? I've always loved making pudding cups for my family in any flavor, and sprinkling them with crushed graham cracker crumbs on top. (I'm looking at you, pistachio, butterscotch, and vanilla.) Throw in some banana slices, and you have a slam dunk. You can substitute the red velvet cake here with the more traditional ingredient — ladyfinger cookies — but I like this variation, especially during the holidays.

- ☐ 1 14-oz. can sweetened condensed milk
- ☐ 1 ½ c. cold water
- ☐ 1 3.4-oz. package instant vanilla pudding mix
- ☐ 3 c. heavy cream
- ☐ Red velvet cake (one round pan worth from a cake mix), cut into small squares
- ☐ 5 bananas, thinly sliced

1. In a medium mixing bowl, whisk together the milk and cold water. Slowly whisk in the pudding mix until the mixture is completely smooth and lump-free. Cover the bowl with plastic wrap and refrigerate for at least a few hours.

2. With an electric mixer, whip the heavy cream until thickened and stiff peaks form. Carefully stir the pudding mixture into the whipped cream and mix well.

3. Now put it together: You can use a trifle dish, or as this picture shows, make individual pudding cups with glass or plastic cups. Spread a layer of pudding on the bottom, followed by a layer of cake pieces, then followed by a layer of banana slices. Repeat the layering, ending with a final layer of pudding. Sprinkle cake crumbs over the top.

4. Cover and let the pudding cups sit in the refrigerator for at least 3 or 4 hours. Serve and go bananas!

The Best Blueberry Pie

So I confessed at not being the most adept "baker," but I do like to make a pie crust every now and then, and this recipe seems to always work well. Yes, you can substitute with store-bought, but I say give it a try. This is the perfect summer dessert. Show up at a friend's house with this beauty, and it'll be the star of the show. Though the pie really needs several hours to set up (even overnight), it's also good warmed up with a scoop of ice cream (yes, store-bought!).

Crust

- ☐ 3 c. flour
- ☐ 2 T. sugar
- ☐ 1 t. kosher salt
- ☐ 8 T. (1 stick) cold unsalted butter, cut into small slices
- ☐ ½ c. shortening, chilled and cut into small cubes

Pie Filling

- ☐ 6 c. blueberries
- ☐ 1 c. sugar
- ☐ 1 c. blueberry jam
- ☐ 3 T. flour
- ☐ Grated zest and juice of one lemon
- ☐ Kosher salt
- ☐ 2 T. unsalted butter, cut into small slices

Glaze

- ☐ ½ c. sugar
- ☐ 1 orange, juiced

The Best Blueberry Pie *(Continued)*

1. Grease a standard 9-inch pie dish.

2. Make the crust: In a food processor, pulse the flour, sugar, and salt until combined. Add the butter and shortening, and continue pulsing until it mixes well and turns into a crumbly mixture. Slowly add ½ cup of cold water, pulsing until it all comes together into a ball of dough.

3. On a floured surface, place the ball of dough. Cut it in half. With a rolling pin, roll both halves into 13-inch circles. Gently place one half into the pie dish and refrigerate until ready to add in the filling. Place the other circle onto a baking sheet lined with parchment paper, and refrigerate also.

4. Preheat the oven to 425 degrees.

5. Make the pie filling: Combine 3 cups of the blueberries and ½ cup of the sugar in a small saucepan over medium heat. Bring to a boil, and then reduce the heat to low and simmer until the mixture is reduced by nearly half, about 20 minutes. Pour the mixture into a large mixing bowl. Add the remaining blueberries, ½ cup of sugar, jam, flour, lemon zest and juice, and salt. Stir to combine, and then let it cool completely.

6. Once the berry mixture has cooled, pour it over the refrigerated crust. Sprinkle with the butter slices.

7. Place the other half of the dough over the pie. Pinch the top and bottom dough pieces together with your fingers to seal the crust completely. Cut 3 or 4 small 1-inch slits into the center of the top pie crust.

8. Place the pie on a foil-lined baking sheet and bake for 15 minutes. Turn the oven temperature down to 350 degrees and bake for 30 minutes more.

9. While baking, make the orange glaze. Mix the sugar, orange juice, and ¼ cup of water in a small saucepan over medium heat. Let it simmer together for about 10 minutes — it should obtain a nice glaze consistency.

10. After the pie has baked for the additional 30 minutes, pour the glaze carefully over the top of the pie and bake for another 10 minutes, or until the top is nicely browned.

11. Remove the pie from the oven and allow it to sit for several hours before serving.

Cora's Salted Sugar Cookies

We all need a go-to sugar cookie recipe in our arsenal, and this one dates back to my toddler years. Our babysitter, Cora, always made these crumbly, slightly salty sugar cookies. They're impossible to roll into shapes, so if that's what you're after, try a different recipe. This just makes really good sugar cookies that I like to pair with a basic almond buttercream frosting. You'll be making them for years to come, I promise.

Cookies

- ☐ 1 c. powdered sugar
- ☐ 1 c. sugar
- ☐ 1 c. unsalted butter, softened
- ☐ 1 c. vegetable oil
- ☐ 2 eggs
- ☐ 4 c. + 4 T. flour
- ☐ 1 t. kosher salt
- ☐ 1 t. cream of tartar
- ☐ 1 t. baking soda
- ☐ ¼ c. sugar, for pressing

Frosting

- ☐ ¼ c. unsalted butter, softened
- ☐ 2 c. powdered sugar
- ☐ ½ t. almond extract
- ☐ 3 T. heavy whipping cream
- ☐ Food coloring (optional)
- ☐ Sprinkles, red hots…go crazy

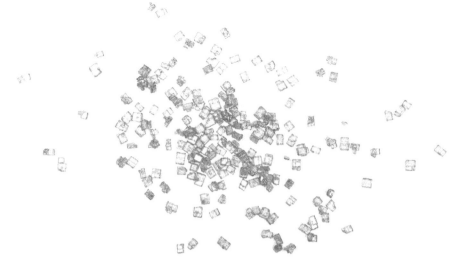

Cora's Salted Sugar Cookies *(Continued)*

1. Preheat the oven to 350 degrees.

2. Cream together the sugars, butter, oil, and eggs.

3. In a separate bowl, mix the dry ingredients.

4. Combine the two mixtures well to create a fluffy, well-mixed cookie dough.

5. Drop by even spoonfuls onto a greased cookie sheet.

6. Pour a small amount (maybe ¼ cup) of sugar in a small bowl. Using a drinking glass with a nice circular bottom, lightly press down on each cookie, dipping the glass into the sugar each time.

7. Bake for 11 minutes, or until the cookies are set and very lightly browned on the edges.

8. Make the frosting: In a small mixing bowl, combine the softened butter, powdered sugar, extract, and cream, to achieve a smooth spreading consistency. Add food coloring if you so choose.

9. Frost the cookies and decorate away!

7-Up® Thumbs Up Pistachio Cake

Now this one really feels nostalgic. I first had this cake when I was a young attorney, at an office potluck. I love anything pistachio-flavored, and it was love at first sight with this fluffy, airy, beautiful green cake. Maybe it's the addition of 7-Up® that really gives it its special oomph... and it pairs nicely with this whipped cream frosting. Deliver in a caftan, and perhaps a nice beehive hairdo, and you'll be the bee's knees.

Cake

☐ 1 box white cake mix

☐ 1 3.4-oz. package pistachio instant pudding mix

☐ 3 eggs

☐ ½ c. vegetable oil

☐ 1 c. 7-up

☐ ⅔ c. chopped walnuts

Fluffy Pistachio Frosting

☐ 1 c. milk

☐ 1 3.4-oz. package pistachio instant pudding mix

☐ 1 large container Cool Whip®

7-Up® Thumbs Up Pistachio Cake *(Continued)*

1. Preheat the oven to 350 degrees. Generously grease two 9-inch round cake pans.

2. Combine all ingredients and beat at medium speed for a few minutes until smooth and well mixed.

3. Pour the cake batter into the prepared pans, and bake for 30 to 35 minutes, or until cake is set.

4. Make the frosting: Whisk together the milk and pudding mix. Fold in the Cool Whip® and stir until the mixture is green and well combined.

5. Frost the first cake layer, add the second layer to the top and then frost the entire cake.

6. If you want, sprinkle chopped walnuts or pecans over the top of the cake.

Amazeballs Chocolate Chip Cookies

I've committed much time and effort over the years to amping up my chocolate chip cookie game to perfect this recipe. If you want more diverse ingredients, go for my Wyoming Whopper Cookies recipe. But if you want to kick it old-school, this is the recipe for you. And don't leave off the salt flakes — they seal the deal!

- ☐ 5 c. old-fashioned oats
- ☐ 2 c. butter
- ☐ 2 c. sugar
- ☐ 2 c. brown sugar
- ☐ 4 eggs
- ☐ 2 t. vanilla
- ☐ 4 c. flour
- ☐ 1 t. salt
- ☐ 2 t. baking powder
- ☐ 2 t. baking soda
- ☐ 24 oz. chocolate chunks
- ☐ 1 8-oz. Hershey's chocolate bar, grated
- ☐ Flakes of Maldon salt for sprinkling on top

Amazeballs Chocolate Chip Cookies *(Continued)*

1. Preheat the oven to 375 degrees. Place the oats into a blender and mix to a powder-like substance.

2. In a medium mixing bowl, cream together the butter and both sugars. Add the eggs and vanilla and mix to combine.

3. In a separate mixing bowl, mix together the flour, oatmeal powder, salt, baking powder, and baking soda.

4. Combine the two mixtures. Stir in the chocolate chunks and grated chocolate bar.

5. Roll the dough into golf ball-sized balls, and place at least 1-inch apart on a greased cookie sheet.

6. Lightly press each ball down with the bottom of a round glass, and sprinkle a little bit of Maldon salt flakes on the top of each cookie.

7. Bake for 10 minutes, or until soft and just starting to turn light brown.

THANKSGIVING

Of all the holidays, Thanksgiving is my family's biggest day of the year, more so than any other. And for decades now, I've taken the lead in the meal planning — setting the menu, and, if I had my druthers, doing most of the cooking. I would be remiss in putting out this Perfect Ten cookbook and not including this special holiday for which I've been making variations of the following recipes for what seems like forever now. If you're in a bind on what to include on your Thanksgiving menu, or what to bring when assigned a dish, this list should cover all bases. Gobble gobble.

Hummingbird Cake

Hummingbird cake…just typing the words makes my stomach start grumbling. It's probably my favorite thing — ever. Really. What is it? Well, its origins are Jamaican, but it's become a southern cooking classic. It's a banana-pineapple spice cake — that's its very broad definition — but this recipe ups the ante, with not just any banana, but blackened bananas (yes, that's a thing!), as well as grated sweet potatoes (giving it a carrot cake vibe), peanuts, and black currants, topped, of course, by a classic cream cheese frosting and more peanuts! It's really the best!

Cake
- ☐ 8 bananas
- ☐ 4 ½ c. flour
- ☐ 1 ½ t. baking soda
- ☐ 1 ½ t. kosher salt
- ☐ 2 c. sugar
- ☐ 1 t. cinnamon
- ☐ 5 eggs
- ☐ 2 c. vegetable oil
- ☐ 1 28-oz. can crushed pineapple, with juice
- ☐ 1 T. vanilla extract
- ☐ 1 c. dried black currants

- ☐ 2 c. roasted, unsalted peanuts
- ☐ 2 lb. sweet potatoes, peeled and grated

Frosting
- ☐ 2 8-oz. packages cream cheese, softened
- ☐ 32 T. (4 sticks) unsalted butter, softened
- ☐ 3 ¾ c. powdered sugar
- ☐ 1 t. kosher salt
- ☐ 1 t. vanilla extract
- ☐ 2 c. roasted, salted peanuts, chopped

Hummingbird Cake *(Continued)*

1. Preheat the oven to 425 degrees.

2. Place the unpeeled bananas whole onto a baking sheet lined with parchment paper. Bake the bananas until they are softened and turn black, about 20 minutes. After they've cooled, remove the peels, and place the bananas into a food processor. Purée, and set aside two cups full.

3. Reduce the oven to 350 degrees. Spray three 9-inch cake pans with cooking spray.

4. In a large mixing bowl, combine the flour, baking soda, salt, sugar, and cinnamon.

5. In a separate large mixing bowl, whisk together the eggs, oil, and banana purée. Fold in the pineapple, vanilla, currants, and peanuts. Now mix in the grated sweet potatoes.

6. Pour the wet ingredients into the bowl with the dry ingredients and stir well. Divide the cake batter equally between the three pans and bake until the cakes are firm and light golden brown, about 40 minutes. Let the cakes cool for about 10 minutes, then remove from the pans and cool completely on wire racks.

7. Make the frosting: With an electric mixer, beat the cream cheese until smooth. Add the butter and mix on low speed, and then add the sugar, salt, and vanilla until combined well.

8. Place the bottom cake layer onto a cake stand. Spread a layer of frosting. Add the middle layer of cake, and repeat with another layer of frosting. Set the top layer in place, and use the remaining frosting to frost the top and sides of the cake.

9. Press roasted peanuts onto the side for garnish (or instead, you can place some between each layer).

10. Serve at room temperature. Mmmm!

Stovetop Green Bean Casserole

I think by now you have sensed that I love the classics, though slightly updated. This one is great — and don't use canned cream of mushroom soup; make your own version! This dish is a bit spicy, so you might want to dial back the cayenne (though I think it's perfect as is). And fried shallots...I really make them all the time and throw them on everything. (You can do the same with jalapenos, red onions...you name it.)

Green Beans

- ☐ 2 T. kosher salt
- ☐ 1 lb. green beans, ends trimmed and cut in half

Mushroom Sauce

- ☐ 1 T. unsalted butter
- ☐ 12 oz. mushrooms, sliced
- ☐ ¼ t. cayenne pepper
- ☐ 1 t. Dijon mustard
- ☐ 2 cloves garlic, chopped
- ☐ 3 T. flour
- ☐ 1 c. chicken (or vegetable) stock
- ☐ ¾ c. heavy cream
- ☐ 1 c. sour cream

Fried Shallots

- ☐ Vegetable or canola oil
- ☐ ¼ c. flour
- ☐ 2 t. cayenne pepper
- ☐ 3 shallots, cut into thin rounds
- ☐ Kosher salt

Stovetop Green Bean Casserole *(Continued)*

1. Cook the beans: Boil water in a large pot. Once boiling, add the salt and then the beans. Cook for only 4 minutes. After 4 minutes, drain the beans and then put in an ice bath to cool them off. Drain again and set aside.

2. Prepare the mushroom sauce: In a large skillet, melt the butter and then add the mushrooms. Season with salt, and add in the cayenne and mustard. Stir the mushrooms well and cook for about 5 minutes.

3. Using a whisk, add the garlic and the flour to the mushrooms, and stir well until all mushrooms are well-coated with flour. Stir in the stock and bring to a simmer. Next, stir in the heavy cream and sour cream and let simmer gently for about 8 minutes, or until the mixture has thickened slightly.

4. Prepare the fried shallots: Heat the oil in a medium frying pan over medium-high heat. In a medium mixing bowl, combine the flour and cayenne pepper. Toss the shallot rings in this mixture, and then place in a strainer to get rid of any excess flour. When the oil is heated (it should sizzle when a shallot is placed in the oil), fry the shallots in the oil until they are lightly browned. Remove the shallots with a slotted spoon onto a paper towel–lined plate, and sprinkle with salt.

5. Put it all together: Stir the green beans directly into the mushroom mixture along with some of the shallots. Let simmer over low heat, for about 10 minutes. When ready to eat, serve with the remaining shallots on top.

Tim's Tried and True Stuffing

I make at least two types of stuffing every year: different combinations of classic stuffing, as well as a cornbread stuffing. This is my tried-and-true stuffing recipe, and it is always gobbled up quickly. I often will double or triple the recipe because it goes so fast, and of course, I want extras for sandwiches all weekend. You can make many substitutions here: leave out the meat if you choose, add other vegetables like broccoli or mushrooms, pour in some white wine, whatever strikes your fancy. Or just follow these steps verbatim and call it a day.

- ☐ 1 lb. spicy Italian sausage, crumbled
- ☐ 8 T. (1 stick) butter
- ☐ 4 c. diced mirepoix (1 1/3 c. each onions, carrots, celery)
- ☐ 1 diced apple (I like to use Granny Smith)
- ☐ 2 T. chopped fresh sage
- ☐ 1 T. chopped fresh thyme
- ☐ 1 t. kosher salt
- ☐ 1 t. ground black pepper
- ☐ 1 t. red pepper flakes

- ☐ 3 c. broth (chicken, turkey, or vegetable)
- ☐ ¾ c. apple cider
- ☐ 14 c. dried bread, cut into 1-in. cubes (I like to use sourdough.)
- ☐ 1 c. chopped dried apricots
- ☐ ¼ c. chopped fresh parsley
- ☐ ½ c. chopped pecans

Tim's Tried and True Stuffing *(Continued)*

1. Preheat the oven to 350 degrees.

2. In a large skillet, cook the Italian sausage. Make sure it's crumbled up and cooked well. Remove the sausage from the pan with a slotted spoon, reserving the cooking grease in the pan. Set aside.

3. Heat the butter in the same skillet over medium heat. Add the mirepoix, apple, herbs, salt, pepper, and pepper flakes. Cook, stirring, until the vegetables are softened, about 6 minutes.

4. Add the broth and cider, and bring to a simmer. Remove from the heat.

5. Add the bread cubes to a large bowl and stir in the broth and vegetable mixture. Add the apricots, parsley, and nuts, and mix well. The stuffing should be fairly wet — if needed, add more cider or broth (or even a little white wine!).

6. Transfer the stuffing to a large buttered baking dish (or two). Dot with slices of cold butter. Cover with foil and bake for about 30 minutes.

7. After 30 minutes, uncover and bake until the stuffing is golden brown, about 20 more minutes.

Not Your Grandmother's Creamed Corn

You have to make this recipe and let it become a tradition. The thought of creamed corn is, I would agree, not always palatable. But this turns creamed corn on its head, and it's the perfect Thanksgiving accompaniment. And ... duh ... how could it not be with Ritz® crackers all over the top? Do it up and make me proud.

- ☐ 2 eggs
- ☐ 2 c. heavy cream
- ☐ 2 T. brown sugar
- ☐ 2 T. chopped chives
- ☐ ¼ t. nutmeg
- ☐ Kosher salt

- ☐ Ground black pepper
- ☐ 2 16-oz. bags frozen corn, thawed
- ☐ 1⅓ c. Ritz® crackers, crushed
- ☐ 8 T. (1 stick) butter, melted
- ☐ 1 T. lemon zest
- ☐ Chives or parsley, for garnish

1. Preheat the oven to 350 degrees. Spray or butter a 13 x 9-inch baking dish.

2. Beat the eggs, cream, and brown sugar in a large mixing bowl. Stir in the chives and nutmeg. Season with salt and pepper. Now stir in the corn.

3. In a separate medium mixing bowl, combine 1 cup of the crushed Ritz® crackers with 6 tablespoons of the melted butter. Stir this mixture into the corn mixture and then pour into the prepared baking dish.

4. Toss the remaining ⅓ cup of crushed Ritz® crackers with the remaining 2 tablespoons of melted butter and the lemon zest. Sprinkle over the corn mixture.

5. Bake uncovered until the topping is golden brown and the dish is bubbly-hot around the edges. If desired, garnish with chopped chives or chopped parsley.

Caramel Apple Salad

This recipe is really kicking it old-school. Cool Whip®, pineapple tidbits, mini-marshmallows … your grandma will/would be so proud of you. I was given this recipe at a work potluck 25 years ago where it got some rave reviews, and now I love to throw it into the Thanksgiving mix. I loved Watergate Salad growing up. This is like that, but instead of pistachio, you get apple and caramel. And kids go nuts for it! Just remember to start it the day before you plan to eat it, since this requires an overnight stint in the refrigerator.

- ☐ 1 16-oz. can pineapple tidbits
- ☐ ½ c. sugar
- ☐ 1 ½ t. white vinegar
- ☐ 2 T. flour
- ☐ 1 egg
- ☐ 2 c. mini marshmallows

- ☐ 1 12-oz. container of Cool Whip®
- ☐ 5 ½ c. chopped Granny Smith apples (no need to be peeled)
- ☐ 1 11 oz. bag caramels, cut into quarters
- ☐ 6 oz. salted Spanish peanuts

1. **Day one:** Open the can of pineapple tidbits and drain the pineapple juice into a saucepan, reserving the tidbits. Combine the sugar, vinegar, flour, and egg with the juice, and whisk together over medium heat. Keep whisking slowly until the mixture becomes a very thick consistency. Add the mini marshmallows, stirring until melted and incorporated into the mix. Stir in the pineapple tidbits. Let cool fully, cover with plastic wrap, and refrigerate overnight.

2. **Day two:** Add the Cool Whip®, apples, caramels, and peanuts to the pineapple mixture. Stir to combine, and keep chilled until ready to serve. (I suggest serving within a few hours.)

Orangey-Appley Cranberry Relish

No Thanksgiving table is complete without some form of cranberry sauce. I know many people swear by canned cranberry sauce, but I personally can't stand it. This recipe is a fresh, vibrant alternative—it's more like a relish of oranges, apples, and cranberries—and a perfect side dish for turkey and stuffing. It is also good on a sandwich the next day.

- ☐ 1 orange
- ☐ 1 Granny Smith apple
- ☐ 3 c. fresh cranberries
- ☐ 1 ¼ c. sugar
- ☐ ½ t. cinnamon
- ☐ ¼ t. ground cloves

1. Squeeze the juice from the orange and set aside. Remove the inner membrane from the orange rind and dice the rind into small pieces. In a small saucepan, combine the diced orange rind with 2 cups of water and bring to a boil over high heat. Let cook for 10 minutes and then set aside.

2. Dice the apple into small pieces (no need to peel it). In a medium saucepan, combine the apple, cranberries, orange juice, orange rind, sugar, cinnamon, and cloves. Bring to a boil and then reduce the heat to low and cover. Let the mixture simmer until the sauce thickens and the cranberries have burst, about 15 minutes.

3. Transfer the relish to a glass dish and let cool completely. Once cooled, cover and refrigerate, and serve whenever.

Gramma's Gumdrop Bread

I have no idea how my mother first came up with this recipe. What I do know is that making this recipe was always a Thanksgiving tradition for the two of us—taking a box of "Hot Roll Mix," making the dough into a wreath, and then attacking it with spiced gumdrops and baking away, adding a nice simple glaze at the end. People always comment on how weird it is and how unique… but it's always the dish that is completely empty by the end of the big meal. I've updated it a bit over the years (welcome to the party, boozy eggnog glaze), and I think this version still embodies my funny and quirky mother's culinary endeavors and offerings.

- ☐ Frozen dinner roll dough (I like the golf ball-sized frozen dough balls)
- ☐ Spiced gumdrops, halved
- ☐ 1 c. powdered sugar
- ☐ 2 T. boozy eggnog (or non-boozy, or you can just use milk)

1. Grease a 13 x 9-inch baking dish.
2. Scatter the frozen dough balls around the dish, leaving just a tiny space between each. Cover the dish with a towel and let the dough balls rise for several hours.
3. As the dough balls start rising, strategically place gumdrop halves in-between, around, and on top of them.
4. When the dough balls have risen sufficiently, bake according to the package directions until lightly browned.
5. Let the rolls cool slightly.
6. Make the glaze: Mix the powdered sugar and eggnog in a small mixing bowl and stir until well-combined and smooth. Add more of either ingredient until you have a nice, slightly runny glaze.
7. Drizzle the glaze over the cooled rolls, and you're good to go!

Judy's Mashed Sweet Potatoes

I know … I've mentioned several times that my mother, Judy, was not known for being a master in the kitchen. However, like me, she had a small trove of recipes that she would come back to year after year, and this mashed sweet potatoes concoction was a favorite of hers—and mine. No marshmallows here—just smooth and creamy mashed sweet potatoes with lemon, vanilla, and maple hints added, and covered with that delectable pecan-brown sugar topping. It's a must-have for your Thanksgiving table.

- ☐ 1 c. brown sugar
- ☐ ½ c. chopped pecans
- ☐ 4 T. unsalted butter, cut into ¼-in. slices
- ☐ 5 lb. sweet potatoes, peeled and cut into smaller chunks
- ☐ 4 eggs
- ☐ 3 T. maple syrup
- ☐ 2 T. vanilla extract
- ☐ 1 T. fresh lemon juice
- ☐ 2 t. kosher salt

Judy's Mashed Sweet Potatoes *(Continued)*

1. Preheat the oven to 350 degrees. Butter a 13 x 9-inch baking dish.

2. Mix the sugar, pecans, and butter in a small bowl using your fingers, until you've made a nice crumbly topping. Cover and refrigerate until ready to use.

3. Cook the sweet potatoes in a large pot of boiling salted water until tender, about 12 minutes. Drain the potatoes.

4. Purée the sweet potatoes in a food processor until very smooth.

5. In a large mixing bowl, beat together the eggs, syrup, vanilla, lemon juice, and salt. Mix in the puréed sweet potatoes. Once mixed well, spread this mixture into the baking dish.

6. Sprinkle the brown sugar topping all over the top. Bake until the sweet potatoes are hot and bubbling, about 1 hour.

7. Let stand for at least 15 or 20 minutes before serving

Mashed Potatoes with Shallots

To me, it's really fun to make mashed potatoes without following any sort of recipe. Once the potatoes are cooked and the mashing commences, I've been known to throw in a multitude of random ingredients ranging from garlic to Dijon mustard to horseradish to sour cream to various cheeses to kale to well,...whatever, really. And it always turns out awesome. (I think a bit of embellishment with mashed potatoes is always better than no embellishments.) I love this recipe. You can make it the day before and cook it (Step 6) before your Thanksgiving meal. And, I really like the addition of two different types of fried onions: red on the bottom, shallots on the top. It's a really awesome dish.

- ☐ 16 T. (2 sticks) butter
- ☐ 5 lb. Yukon Gold potatoes, cut into chunks (no need to peel)
- ☐ Vegetable oil
- ☐ 4 shallots, sliced thinly into rings
- ☐ ½ large red onion, sliced into thin slices

- ☐ 8 oz. cream cheese
- ☐ 1 c. heavy cream
- ☐ 1 t. seasoned salt
- ☐ ½ t. kosher salt
- ☐ 1 t. ground black pepper

Mashed Potatoes with Shallots *(Continued)*

1. Generously butter a large baking dish. Bring a large pot of water to a boil and add the potatoes. Continue boiling and cooking until tender, about 20 minutes.

2. Heat ½ inch of vegetable oil in a large frying pan over medium-high heat. Fry the shallots until lightly browned, about 4 minutes. Remove the shallots with a slotted spoon and transfer to paper towels to drain. Repeat the process with the red onion slices.

3. Preheat the oven to 350 degrees.

4. Drain the potatoes in a large colander. Place the potatoes back into the pot and mash with a hand masher. Add 12 tablespoons (1 ½ sticks) of the butter, the cream cheese, heavy cream, seasoned salt, kosher salt, and pepper. Using hand beaters, mix until smooth and creamy.

5. Spread the fried red onion slices over the bottom of the greased baking dish. Cover with the mashed potatoes. Cover the potatoes with the fried shallots.

6. Cut the remaining 4 tablespoons of butter into thin slices and sprinkle over the top of the potatoes. Bake until the butter is melted and the potatoes are warmed, about 20 minutes.

7. Serve with gravy, if you wish, but they are so good you don't need it!

Best Turkey of All Time

And finally ... the turkey. I've tried many, many iterations of turkey recipes over the years, and this one seems like the one that resonates with guests the most. I think the hints of apple and tarragon help, and it certainly results in a very handsome-looking dish. I have to admit, I skip all the steps that I'm sure much more accomplished chefs/cooks/home cooks display, as in the brining (I buy one already brined), tying the legs together, stuffing the bird, making a stock, blah, blah. I don't do any of that. I clean it, butter under the skin, keep it moist via basting with a glaze or broth throughout the cooking, and voila ... it's done, and that easy. I want to also appease my many vegan and vegetarian friends—you will always see a tofurkey on my table as well!

Turkey
- [ ] 1 12-oz. jar apple jelly
- [ ] 8 T. (2 sticks) butter
- [ ] 1/3 c. frozen apple juice concentrate (slightly thawed)
- [ ] 4 T. fresh chopped tarragon
- [ ] 20 to 24 lb. turkey
- [ ] 12 oz. white mushrooms, quartered
- [ ] 1 large onion, cut into chunks
- [ ] 1 large carrot, cut into chunks
- [ ] Kosher salt
- [ ] Ground black pepper
- [ ] 6 c. chicken broth

Gravy
- [ ] 1/4 c. flour
- [ ] 3 c. chicken broth
- [ ] 8 bacon slices, cut into 1/2-in. strips
- [ ] 2 T. fresh chopped tarragon
- [ ] 1/4 c. apple brandy (or cider)

Best Turkey of All Time *(Continued)*

Prepare the turkey:

1. Make a glaze (this can be done in advance): Stir the jelly, 8 tablespoons (1 stick) of the butter, apple juice concentrate, and 2 tablespoons of the tarragon, in a small saucepan over medium heat, letting the butter and jelly melt together. Remove the glaze from the heat and set aside.

2. Preheat the oven to 375 degrees. Have a roasting pan nearby with a small rack set inside. Rinse the turkey well, inside and out, and then pat it dry with paper towels. Place the turkey on the rack inside the roasting pan. Carefully slide your hand between the skin and the turkey breast to loosen the skin.

3. In a large saucepan, melt 4 tablespoons of the butter over medium-high heat and add the mushrooms, onion, and carrots, and sauté until browned, about 10 minutes. Scatter the vegetables around the roasting pan.

4. Make a flavored butter: In a separate small saucepan, melt 4 tablespoons of the butter with 2 tablespoons of the tarragon. Once melted, work some of the melted tarragon butter under the skin of the turkey breast. Brush the remaining melted butter over the outside of the turkey, and then season the entire turkey with salt and pepper. Tie the legs together with twine to keep the shape (or skip this step, if you don't care how it looks!).

5. Roast the turkey for about 45 minutes and then reduce the heat to 350 degrees. Add 1 cup of chicken broth to the roasting pan and cover the turkey, loosely, with foil.

6. Roast the turkey for about 4 more hours—the turkey is done when it registers 180 degrees on a meat thermometer.

7. While the turkey is roasting, continue to add broth to the pan every hour or so, if needed, and baste with pan juices. During the last 2 hours, brush the turkey a couple of times with the glaze. Make sure to reserve about ½ cup of the glaze for the gravy.

8. When done, remove the turkey from the oven and transfer to a serving platter. Remember to save the juices from the pan. Let the turkey sit, tented with foil, for at least 30 minutes before cutting and serving.

Prepare the gravy:

1. In a small mixing bowl, combine the remaining ½ cup of the glaze with the flour. Set aside.

2. Strain the pan juices from the turkey into a large measuring cup. Add enough broth to this to make 6 cups in total.

3. Cook the bacon strips in a large saucepan until crisp. Pour off the fat from the pan.

4. Add the broth mixture to the saucepan, and bring it to a boil. Whisk in the glaze/flour mixture along with the fresh tarragon, and then whisk in the apple brandy. Let the mixture simmer until thickened, about 5 minutes. Season with salt and pepper to taste.

Index

D

E

Q

R

S

T

V

CPSIA information can be obtained
at www.ICGtesting.com
Printed in the USA
LVHW071316080622
720788LV00016B/573